Advance Praise for *Sr* *Leadership . . .*

Conyers and Wilson provide a POWER-ful resource for tapping teacher leadership within schools to inspire collective intelligence, efficacy, and action that leads to student achievement. Combining research, practical experience, and the voice of teacher leaders, they demonstrate how to leverage collaboration among professionals to transform schools into places of learning for students and adults.

—Joellen Killion, senior advisor, Learning Forward

This book is a must-read for educational leaders who are committed to improving student learning by levering the power of purposeful collaboration. The text combines a strong research base with practical strategies that can be applied immediately.

—Judith Warden, CEO, Blue Ribbon Schools of Excellence

I love this book! This is a perfect text to accompany what we teach in our master's degree in educational leadership. This inspiring and encouraging book will guide graduates in their new roles as administrators.

—Lisa Lohmann, University of Central Oklahoma

An excellent bottom-up collegial focus that provides useful non-technical information about how to insert educationally significant cognitive developments into classroom management, instruction, and assessment.

—Bob Sylwester, professor emeritus, University of Oregon

Breaking the lockdown on student learning—this is the essential guidebook for teacher leaders who remain in the classroom while helping expand collegial knowledge of neuroscience, adult learning and purposeful collaboration.

—Margaret Ridgeway, classroom teacher leader,
Tara High School, Baton Rouge, Louisiana

From a principal's perspective there is no truer belief that purposeful collaboration among teachers will lead to improved lessons and thus translates to improved instruction.

—Priscilla Bourgeois, former principal,
Jefferson Community School, Jefferson Parish, Louisiana

In another direct example of their work illustrating how mind, brain, and education research impacts our classrooms, Conyers and Wilson have nailed it once more. *Smarter Teacher Leadership* is clear and straight to the point: Learning never stops, so why should it for teachers? Highlighting cultural paradigm shifts geared toward entire academic communities, *Smarter Teacher Leadership* is full of insight to improve teaching and learning at any level.

—Michael Fitzgerald, English teacher, Eagle Academy, Eagle, Idaho

We can improve education as we unleash teacher leadership. Marcus Conyers and Donna Wilson have done a tremendous job of collecting the research on the brain, teaching, and leadership that works in a powerful collaborative method that can help us move things forward. Teacher leadership isn't just "nice to have," it is an essential ingredient of effective 21st-century schools where students are engaged and learning. This book will help you get there.

—Vicki Davis, Westwood Schools, Camilla, Georgia

Smarter Teacher Leadership

Neuroscience and the Power of Purposeful Collaboration

Marcus Conyers
Donna Wilson

Foreword by Mary Helen Immordino-Yang

TEACHERS COLLEGE PRESS
TEACHERS COLLEGE | COLUMBIA UNIVERSITY
NEW YORK AND LONDON

Published by Teachers College Press, 1234 Amsterdam Avenue, New York, NY 10027

Library of Congress Cataloging-in-Publication Data

Conyers, Marcus. | Wilson, Donna (Psychologist)
Title: Smarter teacher leadership : neuroscience and the power of purposeful collaboration / Marcus Conyers, Donna Wilson.
Description: New York, NY : Teachers College Press, 2016.
Identifiers: LCCN 2015027649| ISBN 9780807757307 (pbk. : alk. paper) | ISBN 9780807774274 (ebook)
Subjects: LCSH: Teachers--Psychology. | Educational leadership--Psychological aspects. | Educational psychology. | Neuroplasticity. | Metacognition. | Learning, Psychology of.
Classification: LCC LB2840 .C597 2016 | DDC 371.102--dc23
LC record available at http://lccn.loc.gov/2015027649

ISBN 978-0-8077-5730-7 (paper)
ISBN 978-0-8077-7427-4 (ebook)

Printed on acid-free paper
Manufactured in the United States of America

23 22 21 20 19 18 17 16   8 7 6 5 4 3 2 1

This book is dedicated to teacher leaders and the administrators who support and collaborate with them to improve the achievement of all learners.

Contents

Foreword

Teaching and learning are inherently social activities, but too often school culture and teachers' training and expectations leave teachers working in a social vacuum. Yet multiple sources of evidence from education sciences, psychology, anthropology, and social neuroscience underscore the fundamental importance of collaboration in all socially oriented realms of work, especially in education.

Why is collaboration so important in teaching? You could answer this question satisfactorily by simply drawing attention to the technical difficulty of teaching and to the source of feedback, alternative ideas, and strategies that collaboration fosters. You might also mention that teachers' work is emotionally challenging, ever-changing, and intensive—all reasons why the social support received from collaborating colleagues would be welcome. You might appeal to the problematic teacher burn-out and turn-over rates that plague many districts and levels of teaching and point out that teachers with supportive professional networks report feeling happier, less stressed, and more likely to continue their teaching careers.

I would agree with all of these reasons. I would also add another to the pile: By the very neurobiological nature of our social minds, human beings are inclined toward collaborative and cultural approaches to work and learning. Arguably, the evolutionary legacy of our intelligent brain is our social mind; our skills and knowledge are collectively constructed and socially situated. Though of course individuals' thoughts are their own in the sense that they exist in their own minds, individuals' thoughts are also shared with others through social communication, both conscious and not. We learn, take perspectives from, empathize, and emulate one another. Even when we disagree or misunderstand one another, our thoughts and reactions are built and interpreted in a social, cultural space. These statements are all the more true when we consider skill and knowledge domains like teaching, the labors of which are inherently interpersonal. Teachers are people and teachers teach people. It is useful at times to remember that even the basic reason teaching exists as a profession speaks to the dependence of our human mental development on social support frameworks and cultural learning.

With these ideas in mind, jump into *Smarter Teacher Leadership: Neuroscience and the Power of Purposeful Collaboration*. Marcus Conyers and Donna Wilson have produced a clear, practical guide to improving teaching through strategic collaboration. Given the inherently social nature of the human mind and the fundamentally social work of teaching, this book is a useful addition to any ambitious teacher's library.

—Mary Helen Immordino-Yang,
University of Southern California

Acknowledgments

In our work in teacher education, we have seen again and again the transformational power of teacher leaders working in purposeful collaboration with colleagues and administrators to improve student learning. We are inspired by the positive results achieved by educators who earned their graduate degrees in brain-based teaching and teacher leadership and applied what they learned from mind, brain, and adult learning research in their classrooms, schools, and districts. In particular, we want to thank those teacher leaders and administrators whose stories and perspectives are shared in this book: Staci Berry, Diane Dahl, Tammy Daugherty, Pamela Davidson, Theresa Dodge, Mary Leigh O'Connor, Therese Reder, Angel Rodriquez, Kelly Rose, Pam Saggau, and Melissa Smith.

We are also grateful for the input of reviewers Frank Crowther, Mary Helen Immordino-Yang, Joellen Killion, Bob Sylwester, Judith Warden, Elaine Wilson, Lisa Lohmann, Margaret Ridgeway, Priscilla Bourgeois, Vicki Davis, and Michael Fitzgerald. In addition, we received helpful feedback from two reviewers who contributed anonymously in the earlier stages of this book's development.

We greatly appreciate our many dialogues through the years with Mary Buday, starting in 1996 when Donna was chair of education at the University of Detroit Mercy and Mary was Senior Faculty at the National Board for Professional Teaching Standards. Mary has contributed greatly to our work in teacher leadership through the years. We are enormously thankful for both Marys on our team: Mary Buday and Mary Collington keep everything running smoothly as we dig deep into the research for our writing projects. Our wonderful editor, Karen Bankston, helped put the finishing touches on our manuscript and guide it through the production process. Thanks to Lorraine Ortner-Blake for creating the graphics that illustrate key concepts in this text and to Diane Franklin who interviewed several of the teachers whose stories are shared here.

We enjoyed working with Jean Ward again on this, our second book with Teachers College Press, and we appreciate the care that production editor Jennifer Baker and the rest of the publishing team took with our manuscript. And as always, we appreciate the opportunity to work with one another in developing this book. It was a rewarding journey to delve deeper into the practical applications of our ongoing support for teacher leaders who truly lead the way in schools around the world.

Introduction

We stand at a unique point in education. Mind, brain, and education science provides powerful insights on how people learn, and a wide body of research offers a clear understanding about factors that increase academic performance. School systems have a tremendous opportunity to align instruction with such research and, in so doing, to guide all students to develop higher-order thinking skills necessary to be college and career ready. The traditional model of teachers working in isolation is unlikely to be effective in these times when such significant shifts in educational systems are under way. What is needed today to extend the "science of learning" from theory to practice is a system where teacher leaders and administrators work together in a process we call *purposeful collaboration*. One conclusion John Hattie (2012) draws from his review of more than 800 meta-analyses is that

> Accomplishing the maximum impact on student learning depends on teams of teachers working together, with excellent leaders or coaches, agreeing on worthwhile outcomes, setting high expectations, knowing the students' starting and desired success in learning, seeking evidence continually about their impact on all students, modifying their teaching in light of this evaluation, and joining in the success of truly making a difference to student outcomes. (p. 35)

Our work over the last 16 years has been about supporting such an approach, with an emphasis on applying implications of mind, brain, and education research on how students learn—and how teachers can advance their professional practice. In *Smarter Teacher Leadership: Neuroscience and the Power of Purposeful Collaboration* we share key research on adult learning and teacher leadership and shine the spotlight on examples of teacher leaders putting research into practice through a spectrum of strategies. We also share inspiring examples, from the United States and from around the world, of education systems that incorporate principles of teacher leadership and purposeful collaboration.

1

CONNECTING MIND, BRAIN, AND
EDUCATION RESEARCH TO TEACHER LEADERSHIP

The transdisciplinary field of mind, brain, and education research encompasses findings from cognitive science, neurobiology, and educational practice. Students benefit when teacher leaders and administrators work together to ensure that research is applied in each classroom and throughout the school, with a clear focus on improving teaching and learning. This purposeful collaboration can help bridge the gap between research and practice in K–12 education (Hille, 2011).

Mind, brain, and education research provides a conceptual framework to empower teacher leaders with a practical means to support increased effectiveness of instruction across schools and districts. We began our mission to develop and share this framework through a 3-year initiative, Scholarships for Teachers in Action Research (STAR) with the Florida Department of Education. This initiative formed the foundation for graduate degree programs connecting mind, brain, and education research to teacher leadership. To date, some 2,500 educators from all grade levels have participated in the program. A series of impact studies (Germuth, 2012) suggests that what educators learned in their graduate studies has strengthened their teacher leadership and has had a positive effect on student learning:

- In creating and taking advantage of opportunities to align curriculum, instruction, and assessment practices with research on how to optimize student learning
- In designing and implementing professional development to share current research on student and adult learning
- In facilitating a positive, collaborative culture in their schools and districts
- In understanding and modeling best pedagogical practices as mentors and coaches
- In working with colleagues and administrators to design and implement assessments and data collection and analysis with the aim of improving learning outcomes
- In improving outreach and positive relationships with students' parents and other family members, community leaders, and other educational stakeholders to share how we can all support students to achieve their full academic potential.

Our previous book *Five Big Ideas for Effective Teaching: Connecting Mind, Brain, and Education Research to Classroom Practice* (2013b) set out a conceptual framework for increasing teacher effectiveness by bridging research to practice at the level of the classroom. In this text we move to the next level, by sharing insights and strategies for leveraging the potential of teacher leadership through the POWER framework. This begins with an understanding of the tremendous neurocognitive potential of adult learners to develop new knowledge and skills. This potential is of fundamental importance in light of research that enhancing the collective knowledge and skills of educators in turn increases student achievement. Instead of waiting for "born teachers" to enter the profession, new and veteran educators alike need to continue to develop their teaching skills throughout their careers and to adopt strategies demonstrated by emerging research to support student learning. This continual improvement of professional practice requires collaboration and leadership from within the teaching profession.

THE POWER FRAMEWORK

Teaching is an incredibly complex profession, and educators have traditionally been expected to take on a variety of daunting challenges on their own, in isolation from the support and guidance of peers. Some school systems do support professional learning communities and other opportunities for teacher collaboration, but wider adoption is needed. Exemplifying the proverb "Many hands make light work," the shared expertise of teachers working together and with administrators to share responsibility for improving student performance can help make those challenges less intractable and more manageable. Teacher leaders help create opportunities for purposeful collaboration and "call others to action with the aim of improving teaching and learning" (Danielson, 2007, p. 16).

Teacher leaders may emerge from all levels of education and take on a wide variety of roles and responsibilities, all of which aim to contribute to improving students' learning and academic outcomes. Later chapters will present research showing that the most productive educational leadership begins with teachers. Teacher leadership, in turn, begins with effective teaching, but it does not automatically follow that great teachers are great leaders.

In surveys, teachers report two common obstacles that prevent them from embracing leadership roles: (1) a lack of knowledge that those opportunities exist and/or (2) the perception that teachers skilled in pedagogy lack the skills to teach and lead adults (Katzenmeyer & Moller, 2009). Our aim in this text is to help set aside both of those obstacles. In Chapter 1, we define teacher leadership and the many forms leadership opportunities may take—a veritable spectrum of teacher leadership to engage educators of varied experiences, interests, and talents. We also explore research on the impact of teacher leadership on student achievement, school climate, work satisfaction, staff retention, and career opportunities. In Chapters 2–6, we make the case that effective leadership strategies and skills can be learned. We construct a bridge to understanding that what makes a successful teacher can also make an effective teacher leader—and maybe even a happier, more fulfilled human being. This bridge from effective teaching to becoming a positive and productive teacher leader is represented by the five components of the POWER model of teacher leadership and purposeful collaboration:

- *Plasticity and potential* (Chapter 2)—how the brain's ability to continually learn throughout the life span facilitates ongoing improvements in professional practice necessary to make the most of leadership activities. Not only can "old dogs learn new tricks," they can in some ways learn even better than their younger peers, applying lessons from their professional experience to connect new learning with prior knowledge.

- *Opportunities* (Chapter 3)—how to recognize and take advantage of opportunities for collaborating with colleagues, working with administrators and parents, and influencing and advocating for policy changes. Teachers working together have a much greater impact on improving student achievement than educators working in isolation.

- *Work* (Chapter 4)—how to apply metacognitive strategies to working smarter as a teacher and teacher leader. The uniqueness of each teacher's personal and professional background equips her with valuable strengths that can help her develop as a leader and contribute to improving instruction in her school and district.

- *Encouragement* (Chapter 5)—how teacher leadership can help foster a positive, optimistic school climate necessary for change and improvement. Together, teachers can cultivate a culture of success in which educators and students alike are encouraged and empowered to establish and fulfill high expectations.

- *Results* (Chapter 6)—how to learn from successful teacher leadership initiatives in other schools and districts and apply new learning in one's own classroom and school. We shine the spotlight on the good news in education—in the form of success stories from schools across the United States, Canada, and other countries about the gains in student learning that result when teachers embrace leadership roles.

Figure I.1. The POWER of Collaborative Leadership

In short, *Smarter Teacher Leadership* recognizes and promotes the power of teacher leaders to improve student learning, encourages educators to seek out opportunities for collaboration and leadership, and equips them with the knowledge and skills they need to be effective leaders inside and outside their classrooms. We have been privileged through the years to meet many teachers so committed to their profession that they stepped forward to lead and collaborate with their colleagues and work with administrators, parents, and other community members to improve their schools and students' learning outcomes.

In 1999, when we helped develop and deliver training and support for Florida's STAR program, we worked with pairs of teachers from districts throughout the state who came together to learn about classroom applications of mind, brain, and education research. They then returned to their students to put what they had learned to work. They also shared this approach to teaching and learning with their colleagues. Throughout the following year, these teachers met periodically to share and discuss their classroom experiences and their interactions with peers.

This professional development became a launching pad for many of these teachers to pursue leadership endeavors. As just one example, Pamela Davidson, who now works as an exceptional student education (ESE) resource teacher at Treeline Elementary School in Ft. Myers, FL, did a presentation for colleagues at her school and then developed a workshop on the teaching strategies she learned in the STAR program for the Lee County Reading Council. In the years since, Davidson has presented at state and national educational conferences and now mentors new teachers in her school. Davidson also has volunteered to serve alongside other teachers and administrators on committees charged with implementing the Response to Intervention (RTI) program and other initiatives. She says the support she offers colleagues in these leadership roles is as satisfying to her professionally and personally and as important to helping students succeed as her individual teaching. "I have to be at a school where there are opportunities for collaboration and working together as a team," she says simply. "That's where I do best."

TEACHER LEADERSHIP IN THE UNITED STATES

Davidson's is one among many stories that exemplify the benefits of collaboration and leadership and the skills and knowledge teachers need to make the most of those opportunities for themselves, their colleagues, and their students. A middle school teacher in Massachusetts helped form a teachers' book club so she and her colleagues could share stories of using their favorite teaching strategies from texts on effective teaching. A Florida teacher organized "Breakfast with the Brain" sessions for peers at her elementary school, offering healthy breakfast snacks along with an overview of the applications of mind, brain, and education research to classroom practice. In Texas, an elementary school teacher implemented teaching and learning strategies based on mind, brain, and education research that helped her students make significant gains in their reading skills; she then shared those strategies and results in a blog that has reached fellow teachers as far away as Australia. These everyday examples of teachers in action may not make headlines, but they capture the essence of an idea that has the potential to transform American education—the power of purposeful collaboration and leadership when educators come together for the clear purpose of improving teaching and learning. Many more such stories appear throughout this book.

We will also align key aspects of the POWER model of teacher leadership to the Teacher Leader Model Standards (TLMS) developed by the Teacher Leadership Exploratory Consortium (2011). These standards were formulated by teachers, administrators, and teacher educators to further define the ways in which "teacher leadership is a powerful strategy to promote effective, collaborative teaching practices in schools that lead to increased student achievement, improve decision making at the school and district level, and create a dynamic teaching profession for the 21st century" (p. 3).

POWER is an apt acronym for applying fundamental principles from mind, brain, and adult learning research to improve teaching and learning in our schools. Teachers will be able to make the most of opportunities to collaborate with colleagues, partner with administrators, interact with parents, and advocate for the resources needed to optimize student achievement by applying the science of learning. But before we begin exploring each component of that model, let's begin by exploring the many forms that teacher leadership can take.

CHAPTER 1

The Spectrum of Teacher Leadership and Collaboration

Quality teachers who lead and collaborate are deliverers of high-quality teaching.

—Andy Hargreaves, 2015

Purposeful collaboration as an agent of positive school change has a sociobiological and historical basis. Collaboration has always been the way that people get things done. The ability to work together ensured the survival of our species and may have shaped our brain anatomy. Early humans relied on each other to gather food, hunt, and stave off predators. Anthropologists now theorize that evolution favored larger brains; this equipped humans with the ability to negotiate the social complexities of group living—planning and executing a hunt, communicating with and relying on others, and sharing the labors of daily existence (Lieberman, 2013). Humans' social natures, combined with other physiological advantages such as the ability to disperse heat through sweat and the stamina to run long distances, made our early ancestors able to hunt and gather over large territories (and in territories with scant or seasonal plant-based sustenance) as superior pack hunters, able to bring down big game to feed their small communities.

Over time, the human brain became the largest of any species in proportion to body size, developing specialized structures such as the prefrontal cortex to manage executive functions: planning, problem solving, judgment and assessment, decisionmaking, self-regulation, empathy for others, and an understanding of others' points of view. This text will explore how the brain continues to change in response to learning throughout the life span and how much of the input that changes the brain is what we learn from and with others. As in prehistoric times, social interactions continue to be essential aspects of our lives, and brain function reflects this emphasis, releasing "feel-good," energizing chemicals when we are enjoying collaborative experiences and working together to accomplish significant goals. Positive connections and collaborations have been shown to support subjective well-being and cardiovascular health (Cozolino, 2014).

Collaboration guides not only our personal interactions but our civic lives and forms of government as well. Shared leadership in the form of democracy was a grand experiment when the United States declared itself a nation more than 2 centuries ago. The U.S. Constitution provided the blueprint for transferring governance from an elite few to all citizens. This form of government, as Abraham Lincoln so eloquently described it, "of the people, by the people, for the people" has become the foremost model of shared leadership. It works best when we work together, collaborating for the greater good.

In the same way that democracies are only as strong as their citizens' willingness to be informed, engaged voters and partners in governing, schools thrive when teachers step up to take on leadership roles and work together to improve student learning. And when principals and teachers collaborate to lead their schools, they provide a strong model of the importance of shared leadership for students, who are, after all, tomorrow's citizens—of their countries and of the world. This chapter explores working definitions and theories of teacher leadership, the impact that teachers can have as educational leaders, and the spectrum of collaborative and leadership roles for teachers that contributes to improving student achievement.

EVOLUTION OF SHARED LEADERSHIP IN EDUCATIONAL SETTINGS

A common assumption is that leaders are the people at the front of the pack. But in a complex system many stakeholders contribute to the achievement of a shared goal. A variety of leaders bring a shared wealth of expertise, and provide direction and influence progress not only from the front but side by side as collaborators, mentors, and role models. They bring up the rear to identify and provide additional support for those struggling to keep up. Sharing the mantle of leadership optimizes a diverse pool of talents and enables the most efficient identification and dissemination of promising strategies so that everyone can take advantage of advances in learning. As Nelson Mandela once said, "It is better to lead from behind and to put others in front, especially when you celebrate victory."

This dynamic of shared leadership is increasingly evident in educational research results underscoring the importance of administrators and teachers working together to enhance student achievement (e.g., Berry,

Daughtrey, & Wieder, 2009; Crowther, Ferguson, & Hann, 2009; Louis, Leithwood, Wahlstrom, & Anderson, 2010). There is simply too much to do for the responsibilities of leading for change to rest with one individual in each school. Principals today are tasked with managing people (hiring and monitoring the performance of teachers and support staff), facilities, and budgets; reporting to and liaising with the district office; serving as the lead for communications with parents and the wider community; and overseeing implementation of new initiatives and standards. The ultimate aim of all those duties is ensuring that students get the best possible education, but optimizing learning requires a true partnership between principals and teachers. Quality of teaching has a significant impact on student achievement; in fact, it may be the most important factor within schools' control in ensuring that students achieve their full learning potential (Committee on the Study of Teacher Preparation Programs in the United States & the National Research Council, 2010; Tucker & Stronge, 2005). By keeping improvements in student learning as their shared focus, principals and teachers are more likely to enjoy positive and productive working relationships.

So many factors contribute to or potentially detract from school performance that it takes a team approach to make real and enduring progress. A major study on educational leadership notes that "most school variables, considered separately, have only small effects on student learning. To obtain large effects, educators need to create synergy across the relevant variables" (Louis, Leithwood, Wahlstrom, & Anderson, 2010, p. 9). A key conclusion of that report, which was commissioned by the Wallace Foundation, is that "when principals and teachers share leadership, teachers' working relationships are stronger and student achievement is higher," due largely to the existence of a collaborative and supportive school culture:

> Leadership effects on student achievement occur largely because effective leadership strengthens professional community—a special environment within which teachers work together to improve their practice and improve student learning. Professional community, in turn, is a strong predictor of instructional practices that are strongly associated with student achievement. (Louis et al., 2010, p. 37)

Students thrive with the full support of a professional community that brings together the talents, passion, and experiences of both veteran teachers and colleagues just entering the profession, with support and leadership from principals and administrators. When all the members of this community recognize that each professional has something to contribute to leading for change, the immense challenges of teaching so that all students will learn become more surmountable.

DEFINING TEACHER LEADERSHIP

Teacher leadership happens when excellent teachers reach beyond their classrooms to improve teaching and learning for children in their schools, districts, and communities. It is "about action that enhances teaching and learning in a school, that ties school and community together, and that advances quality of life for a community" (Crowther, Ferguson, & Hann, 2009, p. xvii). York-Barr and Duke define teacher leadership as "the process by which teachers, individually or collectively, influence their colleagues, principals, and other members of school communities to improve teaching and learning practices with the aim of increased student learning and achievement" (2004, pp. 287–288). More simply put, "teacher leaders are teachers who transform a learning community—one child, one teacher, one classroom, one school, and one district at a time" (Weisse & Zentner, 2015, p. 243). This commitment by teachers to improve student achievement and school performance can occur at three levels: individual professional development, collaboration and teamwork with colleagues, and active support for positive organizational change in policies, processes, resources, and infrastructure.

Several terms have been used to describe empowering teachers as active participants in school improvement, including *shared leadership*, *parallel leadership*, *distributed leadership*, and *collective leadership*. Whatever the terminology, these approaches tend to share the foremost goal of improving student performance and to recognize that teachers must work together and with principals, administrators, parents, community members, and other stakeholders to achieve this aim. A collaborative approach to school leadership needn't supplant traditional theories formulated to guide principals as the primary educational leaders in their schools but rather apply these theories in a dynamic of shared responsibility (Crowther et al., 2009). A shared vision for collective action can provide the transformational power previously assigned to a single individual. Teachers and principals can work together to identify and implement the most effective strategies for student achievement. All educators on the same team can recognize their responsibility to continue to improve their professional practice and to contribute to a positive and productive school culture. Taking a wider view of transformational, strategic, and educative theories of leadership also supports a new conception of organization-wide leadership as sharing responsibility to improve student achievement._

The word "education" is drawn from the Latin term *educere,* which means "to lead out." In the truest sense of the word then, teachers are "leaders"—in their classrooms, in taking charge of their own professional development, and in taking on collaborative and leadership roles. A teacher leader might act as a mentor to new teachers, supporting them in developing the skills they need to increase their effectiveness. A teacher leader might lead a group of colleagues in the same grade level or in vertical teams, in the process of analyzing student work, planning lessons, or developing formative assessments. Teachers can also lead on specific projects such as implementing new standards or initiating a summer reading program in the community. The formal hierarchy of school leadership puts the superintendent at the top of the district, leading and overseeing the work of principals, who in turn lead and manage their school's teaching and support staff. In this hierarchy, authority is bestowed by position power. But a wealth of research indicates that the most effective leaders in these positions are most successful when they focus on building the capacity of their teams of teachers to increase student learning by orchestrating opportunities for purposeful collaboration and cultivating shared leadership.

IMPACT OF TEACHER LEADERSHIP AND PURPOSEFUL COLLABORATION

Teacher leadership and purposeful collaboration can have a profound and positive impact on students, schools, and communities:

- The link between teacher leadership, the development of collective expertise in effective teaching, and student achievement may be due primarily to fostering a school climate that sets high expectations for students and supports teachers in guiding students to realize their learning potential (Louis et al., 2010). In particular, an analysis of more than a decade of matched teacher and student achievement data found that "peer learning among small groups of teachers seemed to be the most powerful predictor of student achievement over time" (Berry et al., 2009, p. 4).
- Shared leadership among administrators and teachers has a greater influence on student achievement than a top-down approach that isolates responsibility for leading for change (Louis et al., 2010).
- Teachers collaborating through a professional community can help to diminish the socioeconomic achievement gap. A study by University of North Carolina researchers indicates that

disadvantaged students make the greatest gains when their school districts adopt active professional learning communities for teachers ("Study Shows," 2013).

- A collaborative environment, as opposed to schools where teachers are isolated in their classrooms with little time to consult and plan with peers, brings effective strategies and reform initiatives to scale more quickly and helps teachers find solutions to complex problems. As one veteran teacher noted, "I am a better teacher now than I was in my first year of teaching . . . because I've developed my expertise over time—collaborating with colleagues, attending conferences, observing other teachers, reflecting on my practice and working with students who challenge me" (Welborn, 2012).

- A professional community reflects educators' preferences for learning from peers. In a survey by the Center for Teaching Quality, more than two out of three respondents said they rely on fellow teachers more than any other source for support and sources of information about their professional practice (Berry et al., 2009).

- The positive, productive, and energizing school climate that results when teachers have opportunities to learn and plan together enhances job satisfaction and retention. Improved recruitment and retention, in turn, enhance student achievement by keeping experienced, effective teachers in the classroom. In a recent survey, educators cited supportive relationships with colleagues as a major positive influence on their careers. "The teachers commented that their fellow teachers helped them experience a sense of belonging, ownership, and satisfaction in their jobs, even when district mandates and bureaucratic pressures were mounting" (Waddell, 2010, p. 76).

In short, shared leadership and purposeful collaboration support gains in student achievement because these interactions are connected "to the way in which teachers organize themselves into professional communities, to reflective discussions about instruction, and to a sense of collective responsibility for student learning" (Louis et al., 2010, p. 51). As teachers discover the gains that are possible—for their students, for their schools, and for their own professional practice—when they capitalize on leadership opportunities, they are more likely to take on both formal and informal roles and exert their influence to support improvements in learning and teaching, to enhance school culture, to strengthen bonds with the community, and to get involved in policy decisions. Thus, research on the impact of teacher leadership and collaboration is an important topic in professional development and teacher education to encourage educators to take on these roles. As one example, after enrolling in a graduate degree program that emphasized the importance of teacher leadership, 63% of the students completed a survey about the program, and of these, 93% of educators responding said they had engaged in at least one teacher leadership activity, and 70% had engaged in five or more activities involving leadership roles (Germuth, 2012).

APPLYING THE SCIENCE OF LEARNING TO A SPECTRUM OF LEADERSHIP OPPORTUNITIES

By plying an array of strengths, skills, and strategies, educators can engage in a spectrum of leadership opportunities, guided by what we know from mind, brain, and education research to achieve the shared goal of improving student learning. At the core of this science of learning are the truly "big ideas" of neuroplasticity, malleable intelligence, and metacognition (Wilson & Conyers, 2013b). By developing their understanding of these core concepts, educators can progress from using effective teaching strategies in their classrooms to sharing these strategies with colleagues and undertaking other collaborative and leadership roles.

It is important to recognize that while identifying the variety of leadership roles available to teachers suggests the expansiveness of the spectrum, it is also significant that these varied positions, functions, and modes of interacting are fluid, continuous, and overlapping, interrelated and in support of a common aim. Given the complexity of the job of teaching, its practitioners and their students benefit when educators can devote some of their work time to a range of activities such as "working with colleagues on preparing and analyzing lessons, developing and evaluating assessments, observing other classrooms, and meeting with students and parents" (Darling-Hammond, 2010). An examination of this spectrum of leadership roles (Figure 1.1) reveals a wealth of opportunities for teachers to contribute their diverse talents, skills, experiences, and interests toward improving instructional practice and student learning in their classrooms, schools, and districts.

Engage in Purposeful Collaboration

Purposeful collaboration is at the foundation of the spectrum of teacher leadership. Opportunities for teachers to collaborate range from informal discussions and supportive interactions to shared planning sessions to active participation in formal professional learning communities. Research

Figure 1.1. Spectrum of Leadership Opportunities

SPECTRUM OF LEADERSHIP OPPORTUNITIES

RESEARCHING	SUPPORTING	LEADING	PRESENTING	PARTICIPATING	ENGAGING	ADVOCATING	LEADING
Enhanced Pedagogy	New Teachers	Professional Development	Best Practices	in Peer Reviews	Parents	for Educational Policies	Alongside Administrators

Engage in Purposeful Collaboration

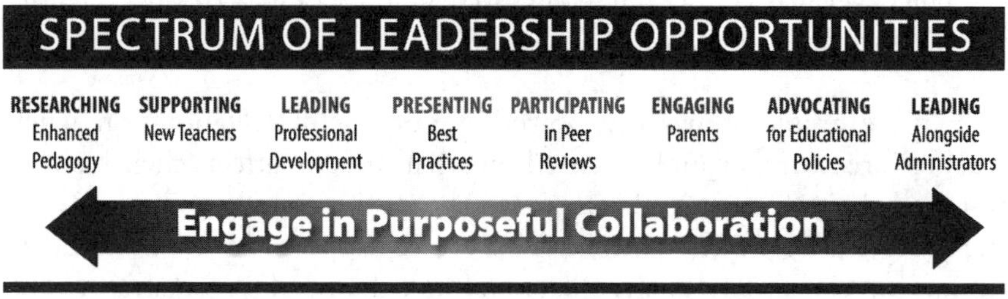

on some of the highest-achieving education systems in the world demonstrates the effectiveness of applying the science of learning through what we emphasize must be *purposeful* collaboration. To work together effectively, educators must focus their clear intent on continuously improving teaching and learning and furthering their understanding of ongoing research into the many interrelated factors that influence students' academic performance.

When teachers combine their efforts to work together toward a shared aim, they are more likely to maintain the motivation needed to persist through challenges, benefit from marshalling their individual expertise and experiences, and recognize when adjustments are necessary to accomplish their purpose. As an example of this "collective efficacy" in action, Costa, Garmston, and Zimmerman (2014) share the story of a team of teachers who decided to collaborate on improving their school's science program, even without funding for materials. The team came up with the idea of organizing science units around a nearby wetlands and working with local experts who were happy to contribute their resources and expertise to support the new program. This type of purposeful collaboration amplifies creative problem solving and distributes the workload of bringing good ideas to fruition. See Chapter 3 for an in-depth discussion on collective efficacy.

A recent comparison of implementations of professional learning communities in two school districts with similar student demographics (Wells & Feun, 2013) provides evidence of the difference between purposeful and less focused teacher collaboration. In discussing the study's results, Fullan (2014) notes that the districts had similar results in teacher surveys regarding items such as "agreement about the need to collaborate" and "agreement about what should be a learning community." But there were big differences on specific questions linking teacher collaborations directly to student learning:

> On questions pertaining to whether "teachers examine and compare student learning results," "teachers discuss instructional methods used to teach students," and "teachers seek new teaching methods, testing, and reflecting on

results," District A had mean responses on a 5-point scale in the 2.17 to 2.44 range, whereas District B responses were in the 3.19 to 3.70 range. (Fullan, 2014, p. 66)

This example shows the power of purposeful collaboration when teachers are more strongly focused on what directly affects their instruction and their students' achievement. The distinguishing factor between these two districts was that the teachers were supported by school leaders to develop capacity to analyze data and link the results of analysis to the personalized needs of their students. Though the study did not encompass measuring changes in student achievement as a result of the professional learning community implementations, "teachers from District B repeatedly showed the researcher evidence of raised student achievement from school and individual teacher results of student learning" (Wells & Feun, 2013, p. 253). These gains in student learning might stem from the district's agreement, top-down and across the ranks of teachers, to keep the focus of teacher collaboration on improving teaching and learning. "The key to generating widespread impact on student learning, then, resides in mobilizing the group to work in specific, intense, sustained ways on learning for all students" (Fullan, 2014, p. 67).

Purposeful collaboration builds on and benefits from teacher leaders and colleagues being metacognitive, reflecting on their thinking and teaching practice, and applying thinking skills we describe as cognitive assets, such as clear intent, systematic planning, monitoring, evaluation, learning from experience, and practical optimism. These cognitive assets, depicted in Figure 1.2, are discussed in Chapter 4, which explores a metacognitive approach to teacher leadership and collaboration. Employing a metacognitive mindset represents a tremendous opportunity for teachers to experience support and a growing sense of self-efficacy that in turn can increase the likelihood of implementing more effective instructional approaches that result in students learning at higher levels.

As an example of purposeful collaboration, Theresa Dodge and her colleagues at Greenfield (Massachusetts) Middle School convened a book study group to share and discuss the teaching strategies from a professional text they had all read that they had found most useful in their classrooms. The study group of 16 teachers and 4 administrators, including the principal, had a far-reaching impact on "whole school and teacher collaboration and creative ideas for teaching students how to be mindful of their learning," Dodge reports (personal correspondence, January 11, 2015). Study group participants conducted a staff presentation the following fall, which led to the introduction of a simple form to encourage

**Figure 1.2. Key Cognitive Assets to Support a Metacognitive Approach
    to Teaching**

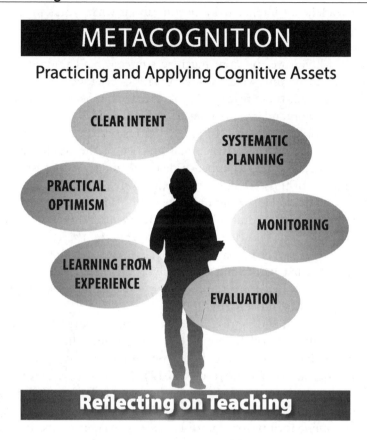

self-reflection that became part of the evaluation process during classroom observations by administrators. The language arts department used content from the book study group as the basis for a nonfiction unit on health and nutrition for the brain.

"Our book club continues to this day," Dodge adds. "It is now mandatory that teachers are involved in one book club. Teachers give suggestions of books that we should read. We look them over and decide which club we want to be involved in. We have around 50 teachers with five to eight different books being read. We meet sometimes during our collaboration times (every Friday afternoon) or staff meetings (every other Monday). Teachers sign up for presentations of our books at the end of the year. Essentially, we went from a small group of 10 teachers reading one book to 50 teachers reading several books."

Engage in and Share Research on Enhancing Pedagogy

Teacher leaders are intellectually curious about what works in the classroom and how best to measure the effectiveness of new strategies. Teachers who embrace this form of leadership are well versed and current on educational literature, on applying new strategies and findings in their classroom, and sharing what they learn with colleagues. As they engage in action research, these teachers "look at data to reflect on the strength of their execution and are unafraid to change whatever they need to in order to improve" (Chang, 2013). Action research by teachers has the potential to improve the instructional practice of the teacher researchers and their colleagues, to enhance dialogue among educators, and to keep the focus of those discussions productively on student learning, to enhance teacher-student communication, and to improve student learning (Painter, n.d.). In addition, when districts and schools facilitate the sharing of this "craft knowledge" among colleagues, these conversations can break down perceived barriers that cause some teachers to feel that talking about what works and doesn't work in their classrooms is presumptuous and pretentious; "a new taboo—against *withholding what we know*—replaces the old" (Barth, 2006).

Participating in and sharing research and classroom results may present opportunities to collaborate with teachers from other districts. One teacher joined in as a community participant in a math project grant through a local university (Germuth, 2012). Texas 2nd-grade teacher Diane Dahl shares stories of successful teaching and learning strategies from her classroom in her "For the Love of Teaching" blog and participates actively in online forums for educators as a way to support and learn from colleagues around the world.

Support and Learn with New and Preservice Teachers

Teachers who are just beginning their careers have a great deal to contribute to their schools and colleagues, suggest Pangan and Lupton (2015)—especially in the area of *relational leadership,* or mobilizing others to improve their practice by forming strong collaborative relationships:

> At the forefront of our thinking should always be seeing new teachers' abilities to provide healthy disruption to school cultures, seeing their ability to guide our community toward more relational leadership, and seeing the unique perspectives that they can provide when they come from strong preparation programs. (p. 129)

When more experienced educators recognize the strengths of their new colleagues, they can optimize their interactions and mentoring relationships. Mentoring new teachers is a common role for teacher leaders. "Being a mentor takes a great deal of time and expertise and makes a significant contribution to the development of a new professional" (Harrison & Killion, 2007). Mentors working with teachers just beginning their careers can provide a variety of supports, from practical tips on time and classroom management and the logistics of navigating in a new school— basic survival skills—to emotional encouragement to guidance in implementing new standards and initiatives. According to Pamela Davidson, the Florida resource teacher we met in the Introduction, "Teachers have a really difficult job, so as mentors and resource teachers, how can we help make their jobs a little easier?" She continues:

> Mentoring entails a lot of encouragement, a lot of listening, a lot of understanding. Then more listening, and a careful approach to making suggestions. One of my first mentees wanted to do literacy centers, but she couldn't figure out how to manage that. I asked, "May I come in and show you some things that I've found that work, so you can see if they will work for you?" Modeling is a delicate thing. You don't say, "Let me come in and show you how to do it." New teachers come in with wonderful and different talents, and they need to know that you respect and care about them. It's just like you do with your students. You have to build a relationship first, so they know that you care about them. The message is: I want you to succeed. I believe in you.

Lead Professional Development

Once teachers begin to step out of their classrooms to collaborate, share effective teaching strategies with colleagues, and mentor new teachers, they may be presented with other leadership opportunities. Educators who studied the impact of teacher leadership while earning their graduate degrees reported undertaking a variety of professional development responsibilities, including developing training for colleagues through an online professional development program, guiding colleagues in the use of new instructional technology, and sharing and modeling the writing of lesson plans under a new framework adopted by the school district (Germuth, 2012). Leading professional development often pays the dividend of improving one's own personal practice via the dynamic of learning by teaching. As the late cognitive psychologist Reuven Feuerstein once said, "As you teach it, you will better learn it" (Wilson & Conyers, 2013b, p. 136).

Take on Formal Roles to Support Effective Teaching

In recognition of the positive impact that teacher leadership can have, some districts and states have created formal positions and programs as a conduit for educators to share their expertise. For example, some districts assign instructional coaches to guide colleagues to differentiate instruction for the varied needs of children in their classroom and to model useful strategies for creating a positive learning environment. In general, research shows that by undertaking formal coaching roles, teachers can guide colleagues to be more reflective about their practice and employ data more productively to improve student learning; in addition, coaching programs support a positive collaborative culture and shared leadership (Aguilar, 2013). In the following chapters, we offer practical tips for coaches and mentors on effective communication and reinforcement of positive, productive relationships with colleagues.

Present at the School and District Levels and for Professional Associations

Many schools encourage teachers to share what works in their classrooms with colleagues in inservice trainings and department meetings. Tammy Daugherty, who teaches 3rd grade at Lakeville Elementary School in Apopka, Florida, worked with her principal to plan "Breakfasts with the Brain," half-hour sessions before school for discussions about brain-based teaching and learning. "We bring in the food, because that helps them come in, and then we come up with a topic of the day and I discuss it. Then they eat and discuss what they think about it," Daugherty explains.

Regional, state, and national educational conferences and their sponsoring organizations offer teacher leaders another venue to support colleagues by sharing research and effective teaching strategies and publishing articles in journals and newsletters. Heather Toner, who teaches English for Speakers of Another Language at Peachtree Ridge High School in Suwanee, Georgia, created a poster presentation for her colleagues at a state conference on teaching and learning principles based on implications of mind, brain, and education research (Wilson & Conyers, 2013a). Many teacher leaders similarly share their learning and as a result develop informal co-learning networks among professional colleagues.

Participate in Effective Peer Reviews

Peer evaluation systems, when effectively designed and staffed, offer several advantages over the traditional model of principals as the sole arbiters of teachers' performance: "Peer evaluators can reduce the demand on administrators' scarce time, provide subjective-matter expertise . . . and enable teachers to take greater control of their profession" (Johnson & Fiarman, 2012). School districts in more than a dozen states have developed effective peer evaluation systems with a key intensive intervention component for struggling teachers (Darling-Hammond, 2013). The program that has become a model for many districts, the Peer Assistance and Review (PAR) program begun in Toledo, Ohio, relies on Consulting Teachers (CTs), veteran educators who undergo a rigorous selection and training process. Consulting Teachers are assigned to work with teachers with subpar evaluations, developing an improvement plan and providing support to help them improve their planning, instruction, classroom management, assessment, and professional development. This form of peer review offers another example of teacher leadership in action, and capitalizes on the expertise of veteran teachers.

Engage Parents in Their Children's Academic Endeavors

Developing relationships with parents early in the school year, keeping them informed, and inviting them to be partners in their children's education throughout the year has been shown to increase student achievement (Henniger, 2012). As the parent instructional support coordinator at Kanoheda Elementary School in Lawrenceville, Georgia, Angel Rodriguez sees his job as providing resources and support for parents *and* teachers. "Suggesting that parents guide their children to think about their thinking and model and use problem-solving skills may open a whole new range of opportunities for family interactions," Mr. Rodriguez notes. The message "work hard, get smart," when combined with sharing learning strategies, resonates with his colleagues and with parents.

Advocate for Policies and Initiatives That Support Improvements in Teaching and Learning

For all the top-down initiatives that aim to improve school performance, from No Child Left Behind to, more recently, implementation of the Common Core State Standards in many states, true reform still must involve the expertise and commitment of effective teachers. "The impetus to see teachers' roles as leaders outside of classrooms provides a paradigm shift in a long-awaited attempt to create meaningful and sustainable school reform" (Boone, 2015, p. 106). In school districts that aim to involve teachers productively in improving policy and practice, educators work together to create a shared vision, to step up and take on leadership responsibilities, to develop a more positive and productive school culture, to put effective professional learning systems in place, to objectively evaluate their progress, and to effect sustainable change. There are even opportunities to contribute to educational policy on the federal level through a U.S. Department of Education program, the Teaching Ambassador Fellowship, in which educators can apply to consult with the department in a one-year assignment (Brenneman, 2015). The fellowships offer full- and part-time year-long appointments for teachers to share their perspectives on educational policy with DOE staff and to provide outreach to other educators on DOE initiatives (for more information, see www2.ed.gov/programs/teacherfellowship/programoverview. html). This program touches on another form of teacher leadership, that of participating in the political realm.

Lead Alongside Administrators

Despite the evidence that teacher leadership and collaboration could have a significant positive impact on student achievement, American schools have been slow to adopt organizational changes that would give teachers the time and impetus to innovate and assume additional instructional and administrative responsibilities—to truly lead from within. "It is time for a bold brand of school leadership, for principals to collaborate with expert teachers who still teach regularly, but who also have the time, space, and incentives to develop their own ideas," argues Barnett Berry of the Center for Teaching Quality in a 2014 *Education Week* commentary. To support this shift, Berry recommends that district leaders should guide principals to identify teachers' expertise and organize their staffs so that educators can work more closely together and make key instructional changes. In addition, teachers need to be willing to embrace responsibilities for collaboration and leadership. DeWitt (2014) suggests that "teacher leaders can be a principal's best asset because they can help mentor and teach new teachers, . . . work as an instructional coach to veteran teachers [and] find the best resources."

The components of this spectrum of teacher leadership suggest the variety of possibilities for educators to effect real and positive change in their own practices and that of their schools and districts. Harrison and Killion (2007) note that "regardless of the roles they assume, teacher leaders shape the culture of their schools, improve student learning, and influence practice among their peers." A primary aim of teachers working together and embracing leadership roles is to enhance collective efficacy, which in turn supports school capacity to improve student learning:

Teacher leadership matters for school success, not just for the teacher who participates in a leadership role. Teacher leadership is a larger organizational construct that extends beyond an individual teacher's roles and responsibilities. It influences student achievement as well as school improvement efforts. The strong positive relationship between the constructs of teacher leadership and collective efficacy promotes success for students, teachers, and schools. (Derrington & Angelle, 2013, p. 6).

TEACHER LEADERSHIP TOOL KIT

This text is a hands-on guide to help educators understand how aspects of mind, brain, and education research support the need for teacher collaboration and leadership and to offer practical strategies for developing skills and outlooks that will be useful for teacher leaders. In effect, it offers a "tool kit" of knowledge, skills, and strategies you can learn and apply in your own professional development and in collaborating with colleagues across the spectrum of teacher leadership. These tools of the profession are explored in detail in the following five chapters, each dedicated to a different component of the POWER framework:

- *Plasticity and Potential.* We are strong advocates of teaching students how neuroplasticity powers their potential to learn (Wilson & Conyers, 2013b). This same dynamic applies to teachers: Understanding how neurogenesis and synaptogenesis support lifelong learning may help surface preconceptions about learning and teaching and inspire educators to take on new learning challenges in both personal and professional life. In addition, becoming familiar with adult learning theories and applications may enhance effectiveness in a wide range of collaboration and leadership roles, including mentor, teaching coach, parent educator, curriculum developer, and team member and leader.
- *Opportunity.* Strategies to make the most of leadership and collaboration opportunities, to optimize teamwork, to apply practical aspects of change theory, and to improve communications with parents, administrators, colleagues, and other educational stakeholders are explored.
- *Work.* By learning and applying useful metacognitive and cognitive strategies to endeavors as a teacher leader and collaborator, a teacher can work smarter and achieve better results. Research is shared relating to the gains that are possible when one

thinks about her thinking and reflects on ways to improve the outcomes of collegial interactions and partnerships with parents, administrators, and others who play a part in improving student achievement.

- ***Encouragement.*** We delve more deeply into the premise that opens this chapter—that our "social brains" reflect human beings' longstanding reliance on others and our benefit from learning and working together. Adopting a positive outlook and developing empathy to understand and respond effectively to others' points of view are crucial skills that can be learned in order to enhance leadership abilities.

- ***Results.*** A teacher leading for positive change may also benefit from honing research skills: to gather useful studies such as those presented in Chapter 6; to learn from and with colleagues new classroom strategies that have been demonstrated to be effective; and to use evidence and data to make decisions and inform instruction. With the flood of information available over the Internet and promoted to teachers from a variety of sources, the ability to assess the validity of the research and professional literature to use in your practice and an understanding of the need to establish credibility as a teacher leader are key skills (Sylwester, 2014).

CHAPTER 2

Plasticity for Powerful Learning Across the Life Span

The discovery of the plasticity of the brain tells us that human nature is more flexible and open to change than has long been assumed. We do not come into the world with a bundle of fixed, stable traits that determine who we become. We develop in continuous interactions with our social and biological environments.

—Walter Mischel, 2014

The idea of a "natural-born leader" is an iconic American image. It's also an idea that we should set aside, with the application of strong evidence from teacher development studies (Darling-Hammond & Rothman, 2015) and from neuroscientific findings about brain plasticity that have been amassing over the last two decades. The reality is that great leaders, like great teachers, are more often made than born. The skills and outlooks that support teacher leadership and collaboration are not innate talents, but learnable skills that teachers can develop and improve at any age thanks to neural processes that power lifelong learning. As Michael Merzenich, a pioneer in neuroplasticity research, puts it, "the brain's machinery is being continuously rewired and functionally revised, substantially under your control, throughout the course of your natural life" (2013, p. 2).

WHAT IS BRAIN PLASTICITY?

The first component in our POWER framework for teacher leadership and purposeful collaboration is the great potential for professional learning and growth grounded in neuroplasticity. When scientists refer to the brain as "plastic," they are describing its amazing capacity to change in response to its owner's experiences and sensory input from the environment. A longstanding assumption was that the creation of new brain cells, called *neurogenesis*, peaked in childhood and early adolescence and then began a steady decline. But animal experiments in the 1990s established that adult brains generate new neurons in response to novel stimuli such as songbirds learning new songs, and advances in brain imaging techniques have since allowed researchers to detect neurogenesis in the brains of adult humans as well (Fotuhi, 2013).

Another process at work in brain plasticity is known as *synaptogenesis*, the creation of synaptic connections between brain cells in response to learning. Neurologist Majid Fotuhi explains that "when you learn something new you create new synapses . . . when you continue to use those synapses you strengthen them"; practicing new knowledge and skills can lead to "measurable structural changes in the brain" as a result of synaptogenesis in just several weeks (2013, p. 26). The neuronal connections that form as a result of learning are referred to specifically as *experience-dependent synaptogenesis*, which underscores that these connections are formed as a result of our one-of-a-kind blend of experiences throughout our lives.

A third mechanism involved in neuroplasticity is myelinization, the production of a fatty substance that forms around brain cells and functions as an electrical insulator, improving the conduction of impulses from neuron to neuron. Myelin is a major component of the brain's white matter. As with neurogenesis and synaptogenesis, research indicates that learning enhances myelinization in people of all ages, which in turn may increase the speed of neural transmission and facilitate our ability to adapt to novel situations and new environments (Lillard & Erisir, 2011). All of these mechanisms are hard at work in teaching and learning; as neuropsychiatrist and Nobel laureate Eric Kandel said, "The whole function of education is to alter the brain" (Sherman, 2011).

TAKING CHARGE OF YOUR PLASTIC BRAIN

The most exciting implication of these discoveries about neuroplasticity is that you can expand your brainpower through learning at any age. Inventive researchers have tested the impact of myriad activities that require mental and physical practice to learn: medical students studying for exams, middle-aged and older adults improving their golf game or learning to juggle, musicians engaging in intensive practice, cabbies spending years memorizing the streets of London, people honing their skills at the game of Baduk, and young and older adults engaging in intensive memory training (Fotuhi, 2013; Lillard & Erisir, 2011; Seidler, 2012; Stix, 2014; Woollett & Maguire, 2011). All of these experiments found evidence of increased neurogenesis, synaptogenesis, and/or myeliniza-tion in response to learning.

Neuroplasticity in adulthood relies a great deal on the "input" we choose for our brains—on the sensory experiences we have and on our mental and physical activities. "Sensory activity is the means through which the outside world influences the brain. Repeated motor or cogni-tive activity can also drive neuroplastic changes. . . . A sustained change in a pattern of neural activity is a necessary trigger for neuroplasticity" (Lil-lard & Erisir, 2011). In other words, mental and physical activity must be repeated and of significant duration to lead to long-lasting changes in the structure and function of the brain.

According to Merzenich (2013), "the average modern human reach-es the peak of neurological performance characteristics in their 20s and 30s" (p. 43), which is good news for the young educators among us! But the rest of us needn't despair, as the neurologist hastens to add:

> Even if you've been sliding backwards as you move past (even far past) that peak, given its reversible nature, your brain plasticity is still there to call on, to engage to help you recover what can be, in a sense, a far more youthful stature. (p. 43)

These findings suggest a variety of ways to stave off age-related cog-nitive decline and, in effect, keep the brain young by "feeding" it with learning:

- **Try something new.** "Learning something new is a fantastic brain grower because it actually requires the development of new synapses, rather than merely the strengthening of existing synapses" (Fotuhi, 2013, p. 119). For example, try a new teaching strategy and share the results with your colleagues. Learn how to use a new technology tool or software to support action research in your classroom.
- **Hone your selective attention.** The brain is in peak "learning mode" when you are alert, motivated, and engaged in and focused on the task at hand (Merzenich, 2013). Focusing one's attention on learning is especially crucial for adults. In lab experiments, "adult mammals only showed such change [that is, neuroplasticity] when they needed to pay attention to learn" (Lillard & Erisir,

2011). Most teachers are extremely busy, continually juggling many competing demands for their attention. But when one is determined to learn, the brain will reward the setting aside of distractions and maintaining focus. Selective attention can be learned and improved.

- **Practice, practice, practice.** Dedicated practice of knowledge and skills results in "changes in millions or billions of nerve cell-to-nerve cell connections . . . [creating] a 'master controller' that can implement this . . . practiced behavior with astounding facility and reliability" (Merzenich, 2013, p. 55). Repetition through practice and the positive feelings of success accompanying learning, which release neurochemicals that support neuroplasticity, help to make temporary changes in the brain permanent. When you engage in persistent practice of a cognitive skill, "you are literally reshaping the part of your brain responsible for that mental task and improving the way it communicates with other parts of the brain" (Fotuhi, 2013, p. 113). Chapter 4 further explores the gains that are possible through deliberate practice.

- **Take advantage of the brain's capacity for mental workouts.** Researchers at Harvard Medical School conducted this experiment: They taught a group of study participants a five-finger piano exercise and asked them to practice it two hours a day. After five days of practice, brain imaging showed increases in the mass of their motor cortex, which controls those finger movements. Then the researchers taught the same exercise to another group but instructed them to practice it only in their minds. Their amazing discovery was that the motor cortex of these volunteers reflected similar changes, even though they had only imagined playing the piano (Begley, 2012). This and other research demonstrates the power of mental rehearsals. For example, a teacher leader could hone presentation skills by practicing a presentation in her mind.

- **Work on your working memory.** The term *working memory* refers to your ability to process information consciously. This is an important skill for teachers, who need to be able to maintain the mental dexterity to process many variables in their everyday practice, such as students' prior knowledge, individual students' moment-to-moment engagement and success with learning tasks and processes, the overarching intent and goal of a lesson, time constraints, interruptions throughout the school day, sequence of activities, and on and on. We often compare the workings of teachers' minds with those of air traffic controllers in that they are dealing with multiple variables throughout their work day. Today, some researchers consider working memory to be the "new IQ" given the central role it plays in many aspects of our lives (Alloway & Alloway, 2013). To optimize their working memory in handling the many tasks of teaching and teacher leadership, teachers should prioritize attention on the tasks that are most essential to achieving goals and that align with clear intent in terms of student learning. No one can do everything. Setting priorities helps steer working memory and keeps one's eyes on the prize of student learning.

- **Seek out opportunities for purposeful collaboration.** Chapter 1 presented the educational research on the positive impact of teachers working together to improve their practice and to boost student achievement. The good news is that stepping out of the isolation of the classroom to become engaged in the professional community will also be good for your brain. Collaboration and social interactions in one's personal and professional life have been linked to less cognitive decline with aging (Cohen & Janicki-Deverts, 2009). Social integration, the feeling that you are part of a community where you are supported and support others, is crucial to optimal social well-being (Keyes, 1998).

- **Take care of your body to nurture your brain.** A wide body of research demonstrates the positive impact of healthy nutrition and regular exercise on peak brain functioning (Conyers & Wilson, 2015). A key mechanism that connects body and brain health is *angiogenesis,* the creation of new blood vessel branches to enhance blood and oxygen flow in the brain (Fotuhi, 2013). It's never too late to reap the benefits of exercise on the brain. Aerobic exercise has been demonstrated in a variety of studies with middle-aged and older adults to improve the brain's executive functions, such as selective attention, working memory, and planning and executing behaviors (Erickson et al., 2014). Another healthy habit that supports neuroplasticity is getting adequate sleep; studies show that sleep deprivation may "downregulate" neurogenesis (Lillard & Erisir, 2011).

- **Minimize stress.** Thus far, we have highlighted factors that have a positive impact on neuroplasticity. But researchers have also pinpointed conditions that may impair the brain's ability to change in response to learning. In particular, chronic stress and depression have been shown to have a negative effect (Lillard & Erisir, 2011). Learning effective stress management techniques is a useful undertaking for teacher leaders.

In combination, these neuroplasticity-enhancing exercises are even more potent. For example, Fotuhi (2013) suggests that "cross-training your cognitive stimulation with exercise and social interaction . . . multiplies the reward" (p. 119). Along the same lines, exercise and social support are effective means of alleviating stress and its harmful effects. Incorporating these strategies into your professional practice and daily life can have a powerful, positive impact on your knowledge, skills, and motivation to take on new roles in teacher leadership and purposeful collaboration.

SEVEN PRINCIPLES OF ADULT LEARNING APPLIED TO TEACHER LEADERSHIP

Understanding and applying the implications of neuroplasticity can have a significant impact both on how educators guide student learning and on how they learn and work together in professional communities. When mind, brain, and education research is applied to adult learning theories, the result—what we refer to as *mind, brain, and teacher leadership*—can strengthen the classroom practice of individual teachers and form a strong foundation in support of purposeful collaboration and a variety of leadership roles for teachers. Remember that our approach is not just about a few great teachers in each school, but a spectrum of leadership across which all can participate. The following principles of adult learning applied to teacher leadership and collaboration can help infuse both formal professional learning communities and less formal networks of teachers within and across schools and districts with a sense of purpose and excitement, the means of ongoing development, and a framework for working toward successful outcomes.

Principle 1: Plasticity Supports Lifelong Learning and Professional Development

Fundamental insights from mind, brain, and education research—that learning changes the brain and that effective teaching practices and a supportive school and classroom environment can have positive effects on student achievement—are also relevant for adult learning. First, as previously noted, we now know from this unfolding science of learning that the adult brain continues to grow new cells (through neurogenesis) and create new synapses (through experience-dependent synaptogenesis) across the life span. These findings have valuable implications for one's role as a lifelong learner continually discovering new ways to improve practice.

Second, key findings about effective teaching practice from the seminal work of Bransford, Brown, and Cocking in the 2000 report *How People Learn: Brain, Mind, Experience, and School* can also be applied to adult learning, specifically to educators' professional development and honing of leadership and collaboration skills:

- **Recognizing Preconceptions:** To ensure that learners can fully grasp new concepts and information, they may need to bring to the surface and set aside "preconceptions about how the world works" (Bransford et al., 2000, p. 14). Many teachers may harbor persistent conceptualizations about the nature of the brain and intelligence that date back to their childhoods—that brainpower and intellect are fixed and unchangeable, that some students (and adults) are "gifted" with high levels of intelligence and others are not, that they either have innately—or can never develop—the skills to become a teacher leader. Before educators can understand the many ramifications of neuroplasticity for their students and for their own professional practice, they must recognize how deeply rooted and long-standing assumptions may obscure their understanding of this emerging research. They can also guide their colleagues to the same recognition when working together to apply new research about teaching and learning to curriculum and classroom practice. Applying and sharing what they've learned about plasticity and learning potential "helps create teacher leaders who feel they actually have something substantive to offer to their peers," in the words of Nevada teacher Benjamin Schmauss (Wilson & Conyers, 2013a, p. 3).
- **Building a Conceptual Framework:** Rather than memorizing disconnected facts, learning new information as part of a conceptual framework supports deeper understanding and facilitates transfer of the learning. For adult learners, understanding the relevance and usefulness of new information—the "why" of learning alongside the "what"—gives them a reason to expend

the time and attention required. In this text, for example, the POWER model brings together important concepts and skills to help teachers progress as teacher leaders and collaborators and to understand the gains that are possible for their students, their schools, and themselves when they take on these roles.

- **Using Metacognition:** "Teaching practices congruent with a metacognitive approach to learning include those that focus on sense-making, self-assessment, and reflection on what worked and what needs improving" (Bransford et al., 2000, p. 12). Critical self-reflection is a central aspect of Mezirow's theory of transformative learning, a conceptualization of adult learning we will explore in more detail in the next section. Self-reflection supports both effective teaching and productive interactions with colleagues, administrators, parents, and other stakeholders in improving student learning. The gains that are possible from applying a metacognitive approach to teacher leadership and collaboration underscore a theme that runs throughout this text.

Principle 2: Intelligence Is Malleable and Multifaceted

With knowledge in place about the brain's plasticity, teacher leaders can better understand and apply the corollary that adult intelligence is malleable and multifaceted. Accepting that they have the brainpower to learn new strategies and skills throughout their careers can help teachers achieve what educational researcher John Mezirow (1990) called *transformative learning*, the process of "reassessing the presuppositions on which our beliefs are based and acting on insights derived from the transformed meaning perspective that results from such reassessments" (p. 18). Supported by experience-dependent synaptogenesis, teachers can learn new strategies from and with their peers and develop skills to facilitate purposeful collaboration and leadership. Adopting a new mindset that intelligence is malleable and that we can all learn a variety of skills can help set aside limiting perceptions such as "I'm not a technology person" and "That's the way I was taught, so that's the way I'm going to teach."

Incorporating the implications of neuroplasticity and malleable intelligence into our professional practice will likely involve restructuring our schema about learning and teaching, which can be "the hardest learning for most adults" (Knowles, Holton, & Swanson, 2005, p. 191). Changing our schema involves what has been described as "double-loop learning" so that we can recognize when new concepts conflict with what we think we know, test these new concepts to ensure that they are superior to our existing mental models, and construct new mental models that incorporate these concepts into our professional practice (Knowles et al., pp. 190–191). This type of learning entails developing the metacognitive ability of what Schon (1987) refers to as *reflection-in-action,* or developing awareness of our existing mental models and testing them against new ideas and teaching strategies to determine whether they need to be replaced or can be improved.

The need for self-awareness of our existing schema and ongoing self-reflection is at the core of adult learning theory, which recognizes that, for better and for worse, we are shaped by our experiences. "As we accumulate experience, we tend to develop mental habits, biases, and presuppositions that tend to cause us to close our minds to new ideas, fresh perceptions, and alternative ways of thinking" (Knowles et al., 2005, p. 66). Developing a metacognitive approach to our professional practice and learning in collaboration with peers can help us continually recognize what among our knowledge, attitudes, and experiences remains useful and relevant and what we might need to change.

Mezirow began his research on adult learning in the 1970s, studying the learning processes and pathways of women reentering university programs and careers following long gaps in their education or work history. Those who made successful transitions worked their way through several phases: confronting a dilemma that moved them to action; assessing fundamental assumptions; recognizing that others have successfully negotiated the same changes they are going through; exploring options for new roles, relationships, and actions; planning a course of action; acquiring the skills and knowledge needed to implement their plans; provisionally trying out their new roles; and building competence and self-confidence in their new roles and skills (Kitchenham, 2008). In short, they transformed themselves professionally through learning.

Mezirow's theory of adult learning through transformation can be directly applied to the new frames of reference teachers need to develop in embracing purposeful collaboration and leadership roles. Although learning and incorporating new information into one's practice is crucial in transformative learning, this model of adult learning also incorporates the ongoing development of cognitive, emotional, reflective, and social capacities. Through transformative learning, teachers can come to see themselves as agents of change in improving student achievement in their classrooms, schools, and districts (Lysaker & Furuness, 2011). This recognition of and acceptance of the need for transformation allows teachers to develop new capabilities they can use to continuously adapt to new challenges and opportunities in their classrooms, schools, and profession. As just one example, the new science of learning undergirding professional teaching practice provides a natural vehicle for looking at the potential of individual students in a different and more productive light.

Another model of adult learning, Robert Kegan's constructive-developmental theory, also examines learning as a transformative process, exploring how people change the way they make meaning of new information and deal with complexity, multiple demands, and uncertainty in their personal and work lives (Kegan, 2000). Kegan proposed a progression of how humans *construct* reality, from childhood to full maturity, and how those social, emotional, and cognitive constructs *develop* to more complex levels over time—as Berger (2003) puts it, "as we increase our capacity to take perspectives, view authority in new ways, and see shades of grey where we once saw only black and white" (p. 1). Kegan's model, which has been extensively applied to educational leadership (see the discussion under Principle 3), is consistent with mind, brain, and education research on the malleability of intelligence throughout the life span. In their research on guiding adults to embrace positive change in the workplace, Kegan and Lahey found that many individuals "were able to evolve whole patterns of increasingly complex and agile ways of apprehending the world" (2009, Preface and Acknowledgments).

Principle 3: Each Adult Brain Is Unique

The power of teacher leadership derives, in large part, from the diverse talents, skills, and collective expertise that educators working together bring to bear. No one can be a genius at everything, but through purposeful collaboration, teachers gain access to a treasure chest of strategies and ideas about what works in the classroom and support for evaluating and implementing the most successful among them. A teacher who is especially creative at lesson planning may work alongside another who is an excellent data analyst. Through collaboration, each can benefit from the other's expertise and develop and share strengths. As Merzenich notes:

> If you think of the million and one things that you know, and that you can do—that no one else on the planet knows or does in exactly the same ways—you can begin to understand how unique you are. (2013, p. 16)

In our presentations with educators, we use the metaphor that each brain is as unique as a fingerprint, reflecting the totality of what each person has learned and experienced up to that point in his or her life. Based on your classroom teaching experiences, teacher training, and efforts to improve your professional practice by studying the research and gathering and employing new strategies from educational literature, online resources, and workshops and conferences, you have your own strengths, ideas, perspectives, and body of work to contribute to your professional community.

Not only is your brain wholly individual, but your "ways of knowing," to use the terminology of Kegan's constructive-developmental framework of adult learning, may also differ from those of your colleagues and administrators. In her work on adult educational leadership, Ellie Drago-Severson (2008, 2010) explores how educators with differing developmental orientations might widen their own perspectives and collaborate more effectively with colleagues:

- Educators with an *instrumental* way of knowing tend to be concrete thinkers who appreciate the order imposed by following rules. They "feel supported when others provide specific advice and explicit procedures so that they can accomplish their goals" (Drago-Severson, 2008, p. 61). Those who tend toward an instrumental way of knowing might benefit by being more open to suggestions from colleagues and administrators about other "right" ways of doing things and by stretching to think more abstractly.

- Educators with a *socializing* way of knowing are more comfortable with abstract thinking and considering others' opinions—to the point that they may subordinate their needs and preferences to those of others. Drago-Severson suggests that colleagues and supervisors can best support teachers who tend toward a socializing way of knowing by "encouraging them to share their perspectives about pedagogy, student work, and policies in pairs or small groups before sharing them with a larger group" to help them clarify and solidify their values and standards (2008, p. 61). A person who feels overly sensitive to others' opinions might benefit from focusing on accepting that others may have conflicting viewpoints that don't necessarily negate one's own or threaten working relationships.

- Kegan's formulation of the *self-authoring* way of knowing holds that people with this developmental orientation have assimilated others' perspectives, opinions, and rule-making systems into their own self-governing approach. At the same time, people with this orientation may have difficulty opening up to opposing points of view and may benefit from accepting that they can learn from their colleagues.

In short, "a person's way of knowing shapes how she understands her role and responsibilities as a teacher, leader, and learner, and how she thinks about what makes a good teacher, what makes a good leader, what constitutes effective teaching practice" (Drago-Severson, 2008, p. 61). Applying what we know about plasticity and malleable intelligence, we can see that we and our colleagues are not locked into these ways of knowing. Rather, we have the capacity to build on the strengths of these orientations and to continue to enhance our ability to learn from and with our colleagues and, in doing so, to steadily improve our individual and collective professional practice by making the most of all of the unique brains in our professional communities.

Principle 4: A Positive School Environment Supports Positive Change

A crucial responsibility of teacher leaders is "developing a positive climate and a collective responsibility in a community environment, ultimately benefiting students" (Weisse & Zentner, 2015, p. 238). A positive school culture—characterized by collegiality and trust, shared responsibility for student learning, collective commitment to improvement, opportunities for collaboration, and the belief that all students can learn—amplifies both teacher and student motivation and improves school effectiveness (Peterson & Deal, 2009). While principals must take the lead in fostering a positive and productive environment, teachers have a significant impact on school climate in both formal and informal roles as "keepers of the values who socialize new hires, . . . storytellers who keep history and lore alive, and heroines and heroes who act as exemplars of core values" (Peterson & Deal, 2009, pp. 8–9). Educators just starting their careers can contribute significantly to a positive school culture: "Beginning teachers enter the profession unclouded and joyful about the potential for making a difference in the world, and this enthusiasm, if welcomed, can have a profound impact on school culture" (Pangan & Lupton, 2015, p. 124).

At the center of a positive school environment is an optimistic outlook, a shared belief that students can learn when provided with effective instruction and that teachers can continually improve their professional practice to provide that instruction. The good news is that optimism can be learned and enhanced. Like intelligence, your proclivity toward positive or negative thinking is not a fixed trait. Seligman (2011a) reports that a program to train teachers to apply techniques that emphasize an optimistic outlook in their personal and professional lives had a positive effect on their students. In addition, strategies to support resilience and optimism across an organization, including honing people's strengths and fostering strong relationships, are core competencies for leaders,

Seligman suggests. One aspect of optimism is being motivated and persistent in the face of tough problems, which is certainly a valuable trait for teachers! We will delve more deeply into the power of practical optimism for teacher leaders in Chapter 5.

When schools are designed to optimize collegiality and positive support among teachers, students and teachers alike benefit. Characteristics of a collegial school culture include teachers talking about their professional practice and sharing strategies and ideas with colleagues, teachers observing each other in the classroom, and "educators rooting for one another's success" (Barth, 2006). Drago-Severson (2012) suggests that school culture may also be enhanced when principals can take advantage of interactions with their peers:

> These school leaders explained that they yearn for regular, ongoing opportunities to reflect with colleagues and fellow principals on the challenges of leadership, emphasizing that this type of ongoing collegial reflection would help them to more effectively exercise leadership, avoid burnout, and renew themselves. Although all these principals spontaneously voiced the desire to engage in collegial reflection, only 3 were doing so on a regular basis. This research suggests the importance of supporting and retaining principals by using reflection and collegial support for renewal, with serious implications for education policy and school district practices.

Principle 5: Teacher Leaders Learn Through Purposeful Inquiry

In our work in teacher education, two practical strategies we share for engaging students are to provide hands-on activities to support their learning whenever possible and to give students choices in what they read and research. The same dynamics are true for adult learners: They are more likely to do the work required to learn when they see that new knowledge and skills will help them solve problems or improve their personal and/or professional lives. As Knowles and colleagues explain:

> Adults are motivated to learn to the extent that they perceive that learning will help them perform tasks or deal with problems that they confront in their life situations. Furthermore, they learn new knowledge, understandings, skills, values, and attitudes most effectively when they are presented in the context of application to real-life situations. (2005, p. 67)

Action research provides a means for teacher leaders to seek out new ideas and strategies to improve their teaching, to try out those strategies in their classrooms, to analyze their effectiveness and adapt them as necessary, and to share their results with colleagues. This form of practical research can be a conduit to educational studies and strategies that address the needs of specific students in a diverse classroom and to teaching approaches that can help educators comply with new standards and curricular requirements (Sagor, 2000).

Action research can also be extremely motivating and rewarding for teachers and provides a pathway to collaboration and leadership opportunities. This practical research involving new teaching strategies and sharing what one has learned with colleagues is a prime example of experiential learning, a form of learning especially attuned to the needs and preferences of adult learners. Experiential learning is characterized by concrete experience and testing of new ideas, observations and reflection, and the opportunity to form new abstract concepts and generalizations (Kolb, 1984). Arizona middle school teacher Chuck Balogh says classroom research he conducted to assess the impact on learning of guiding students to adopt a more optimistic outlook "has turned into a passion for me." Massachusetts teacher Theresa Dodge has incorporated aspects of action research into her daily practice as a way to evaluate the effectiveness of lessons and make changes when necessary. "I have to constantly adjust who I am as a teacher to fit the situation at hand," Dodge says. "It is a continuous process, much like putting a puzzle together every day. I love puzzles" (Wilson & Conyers, 2013a).

Principle 6: Collaboration Enhances Learning for Teacher Leaders

Teaching is often an isolated profession, yet educators have tremendous potential to learn together and to benefit from collegial support in implementing effective teaching strategies, assessing the impact of those approaches, and identifying likely solutions to perplexing classroom challenges. As we have noted previously, teachers rely on their colleagues more than any other source for information, strategies, and suggestions for improving their practice. This collaborative learning occurs in everyday interactions, in formal learning communities and professional development, and in a variety of online forums. Opportunities for collaboration and shared leadership are the hallmark of innovative organizations; in addition, working with colleagues to agree on the objectives and means of enhancing professional practice is considered a best practice in adult learning (Knowles et al., 2005).

For example, teachers who earned their degrees in an online program say they benefit from learning with educators in their cohorts from across the country (Wilson & Conyers, 2013a). "You learn about what's going on in classrooms in California, North Carolina, and Georgia. You find out there are a lot of issues that we're all having problems with, and we share ideas about what we're doing," says Florida teacher Tammy Daugherty. "I like to talk shop, and I love teaching, so here I am with 20 to 25 other people who like to talk about teaching and learning." Or, as Georgia elementary teacher Melissa Smith puts it, "As soon as you start sharing ideas with others, they get bigger and better."

To optimize the impact of purposeful collaboration, teachers and administrators should work together to establish a supportive school culture where the traits of caring, cooperation, and intellectual curiosity about effective teaching practice are valued (Smith, Wilson, & Corbett, 2009). Practical aspects of strong collaborative learning communities include:

- scheduling extended blocks of time during the school day for teachers to engage in distraction-free, deep discussions about their practice;
- guiding the group to develop its own guidelines for staying on topic, encouraging active participation by all teachers, and other norms to make the most of their time together; and
- training internal facilitators (Smith et al., 2009).

Principle 7: Teacher Leaders Put What They've Learned to Work

Teachers are trained and experienced in pedagogical practice, or educating children. In contrast, the field of *andragogy,* the study of teaching adult learners, acknowledges that adult learning differs from children's learning in several ways that have significance for your own professional learning, collaboration with colleagues, and roles as a mentor, coach, and teacher leader. The late Malcolm Knowles, acknowledged as a leader in the field of andragogy, and colleagues (Knowles et al., 2005) developed these assumptions about adult learners that form the basis of the andragogical model, applied here to teachers learning in professional communities and taking on leadership roles:

- Adult learners have a compelling "need to know" why and how learning new skills and knowledge will benefit their professional practice. When you are coaching and mentoring peers, for example, they will be more motivated, open, and interested in working with you if you can make a compelling case for how your interactions might improve their teaching and make classroom challenges more manageable. This is similar to students wanting to know, "Why do we need to learn this?"

- We talk a lot in education about guiding students to become self-directed learners. This concept of taking charge of one's learning is at the core of andragogy: "Adults have a self-concept of being responsible for their own decisions, for their own lives" (Knowles et al., 2005, p. 65). Like other adults, when confronted with mandatory training and requirements for learning new standards and classroom practices that are thrust upon them, teachers may be resistant. On the other hand, when teachers are invited to help shape the objectives of their professional development and have input into implementing new standards, that sense of ownership encourages buy-in and more enthusiastic and productive participation. In a study of collaborative learning communities in New Jersey, teachers agreed that voluntary participation enhanced engagement among colleagues and improved outcomes (Smith et al., 2009).

- Adult learners have a greater range of experiences than children, and these experiences influence their learning. These diverse experiences make teachers learning together "more heterogeneous in terms of background, learning style, motivation, needs, interests, and goals"; as a result, "the richest resources for learning reside in the adult learners themselves" (Knowles et al., 2005, p. 66). In other words, mentors and colleagues should acknowledge their peers' experiences and value their contributions. But at the same time, each member of the learning community should be encouraged and guided to consider whether the mental models and schema of professional practice borne of those prior experiences interfere with learning important new concepts and integrating new research and strategies into practice.

- Learning motivation is related to adults' readiness and orientation to learn and act on new concepts and knowledge. An example of the issue of readiness can be found in mentoring new teachers; many join the profession full of enthusiasm and learning of the latest educational research, but they benefit from guidance and support as they "learn in place" to manage the complexities of the classroom. And most will appreciate the opportunity to talk through challenges rather than struggling in isolation. In terms of orientation, opportunities for collaborative learning should acknowledge that teachers, like other adults, "are motived to learn to the extent that they perceive that learning will help them perform tasks or deal with problems that they confront in their life situations" (Knowles et al., 2005, p. 67).

A unifying principle in the research on teacher collaboration and leadership and adult learning is the need for educators, like their students, to sense that what they are learning is practical and useful. They should be able to apply immediately what they're learning about new standards and teaching strategies to practice in their classroom. In addition, opportunities for purposeful collaboration and teacher leadership should capitalize on what educators have to contribute and emphasize the practical impact on improving student achievement at the heart of these endeavors. In the next chapter, we explore what skills and knowledge you can build in your professional practice to make the most of opportunities to enhance the collective capacity of your school and district.

CONSTRUCTIVE CONCLUSIONS: THE POWER OF PLASTICITY IN TEACHER LEADERSHIP

Applying what we now know, thanks to research ranging from neuroscience to adult learning theory, we can see that all teachers—even those who have worked for years in isolation from their peers—have the capacity to learn new skills and outlooks that will be useful in purposeful collaboration and teacher leadership. Here are three strategies to help make the most of your brain's neuroplasticity:

Become more "mindful" of the important tasks at hand. There's been a lot of interest in recent years in the advantages of developing mindfulness—and with good reason. The ability to pay attention on purpose and to stay in the moment, rather than being distracted by nonproductive thoughts or allowing your mind to be pulled in many different directions, is a crucial aspect of developing your selective attention and enhancing working memory. You may pride yourself on your ability to multitask, but your brain learns much more efficiently and effectively when you concentrate on one thought at a time. In fact, research suggests that the brain is not designed to handle two tasks simultaneously, although it can shift quickly from thought to thought or from action to action (Hamilton, 2008).

Many mental health professionals advocate for learning to meditate and building a few moments for quiet reflection into your daily routine, and school psychologists have begun to study the benefits of developing mindfulness in the school setting (Felver, Doerner, Jones, Kaye, & Merrell, 2013). Even in the midst of a hectic school day, you can train your brain to block out myriad distractions and focus on the idea or task that is most important at that moment. A common exercise for training your brain to be more mindful is to focus on your breathing for one minute. Take a deep breath and let it out slowly. Clear your thoughts and focus only on the act of breathing in and out. By learning to be mindful in this way, you can better transfer that ability to focus your attention on an idea exchange with a colleague, a conversation with an administrator or parent, or the design of an action research project.

Forge purposeful connections with colleagues. We will explore in more detail in the next chapter skills and strategies that can help optimize your interactions with fellow teachers, administrators, parents, and other educational stakeholders. For now, it might be helpful to emphasize brain and adult-learning research in support of purposeful collaboration: When teachers work together to tackle the challenges they confront in their classrooms every day, they bring to bear the combined power of all of their unique brains and varied professional experiences and perspectives. Social learning is an effective means of furthering your professional knowledge and practice.

Build physical activity into your daily schedule. What's good for the body is great for your brain. Regular exercise improves brain function and reduces stress. A brisk walk during your lunch break can help to re-energize your thinking and enthusiasm for teaching. If your schedule does not permit a mid-day break, building physical activity into your schedule before or after the school day can help keep your body and brain in peak operating condition.

CHAPTER 3

Opportunities for Teacher Collaboration

Harnessing the Power of the Social Brain

A grand dream doesn't become a significant reality through the actions of a single person. It requires a team effort. It requires solid trust and strong relationships. It requires deep competence and cool confidence. It requires group collaboration and individual accountability.

—James Kouzes & Barry Posner, 2012

Around the world high-performing education systems focus on teachers working together for positive change. They are creating more effective lessons, evaluating student learning, supporting instructionally useful formative assessment, and learning with and from one another to enhance their professional practice—all with a single-minded focus on improving student outcomes. As discussed in Chapter 1, research shows that regular opportunities to collaborate and consult with one another make good teachers great and lower-ability teachers better. "Talking to peers about the complex task of instructing students is an integral part of every teacher's job and results in rising student achievement" (Leana, 2011, para. 1, under "Applying Research to Practice"). In fact, beyond an initial focus on teacher selection, long-term support for collaboration and a distributed leadership approach make the most difference in students' learning gains.

Though teachers spend much of the school day on their own with their students in the classroom, advances in their own professional practice and in that of their peers can be attributed in large part to what they learn from each other in sharing effective strategies, relaying useful research, and puzzling through challenges as a team. "The work of improving practice must therefore be conceptualized as collective rather than individual" (Darling-Hammond, 2013, p. 107).

In light of these findings, a critical skill for teacher leaders, suggests Danielson (2007), "is the ability to collaborate with others. Teacher leaders must enlist colleagues to support their vision, build consensus among diverse groups of educators, and convince others of the importance of what they are proposing and the feasibility of their general plan for improvement" (p. 15).

Thus, the second component of our POWER framework focuses on creating opportunities for purposeful collaboration and making the most of those opportunities. This chapter explores research and recommendations on how teachers can build their collective capacity, make the most of social learning to enhance their professional practice, and advocate to build time into the school day for productive interactions with peers to consult, observe, and share ideas. As Hargreaves and Fullan (2012) note, "teaching like a pro means planning teaching, improving teaching, and often doing teaching not as an isolated individual but as part of a high-performing team. It means developing shared professional capital with an organization and community" (p. 22).

BUILDING COLLECTIVE CAPACITY TO ENHANCE STUDENT LEARNING

The concept of *social capital* was first put forth by sociologist James Coleman (1988) to investigate how groups of people (e.g., families, schools, and communities) in relationships that exhibit high degrees of trust can work together to share information efficiently and optimize available resources. In effect, the whole can truly be more than the sum of its parts when an organization has high social capital. This idea has been widely applied in educational research in the teacher surveys described by Leana (2011), for example, and in studies by Goddard, Hoy, and Hoy (2004) about the significant impact that the collective efficacy of teachers in a school can have on student achievement. *Collective efficacy* refers to a shared belief that teachers working together can make a lasting difference in their students' lives—much more so than teachers working alone in their classrooms and isolated from colleagues.

Related to these education-specific findings is research from a variety of business settings that colleagues who develop the skills to work together effectively can enhance their *collective intelligence*. Social scientists observing patterns and outcomes in work teams have found that groups exhibiting effective internal dynamics actually perform on a higher intellectual plane than the cognitive capacities of individual team members taken together (Pentland, 2014; Woolley, Chabris, Pentland, Hashmi, & Malone, 2010). Groups exhibiting more extensive collective intelligence are adept at conversational turn taking (rather than one person dominating the discussion) and share higher levels of social sensitivity (that is, team members are attuned to others' emotions). The researchers theorized that the combination of conversational turn taking and sensitivity to others' emotional responses facilitates the flow of diverse ideas and responses to those ideas that are necessary for efficient group problem solving.

Thus, there is a great deal of evidence that purposeful collaboration can provide a pathway to effective school improvement. Too often, though, DuFour and Fullan (2013) contend, school policies emphasize and reward developing the talent of individual teachers. This focus on "human capital" approaches tends to divide teachers, engendering hierarchies of influence, respect, and privilege. Far more productive and ultimately beneficial to students are those systems and policies that value teachers working together to realize a greater return in the form of social capital. "Teacher effectiveness has less to do with individual attributes, and far more to do with the extent to which teachers work with each other and provide collective leadership for their schools and communities" (Berry, Daughtrey, & Wieder, 2009, p. 2).

In schools where educators work together to parlay social capital into collective capacity for more effective teaching, teachers view ongoing learning as a fundamental aspect of their jobs. The climate in these schools is marked by collegiality and a shared commitment to continuous improvement of professional practice (Feiman-Nemser, 2012). The daily schedule provides regular opportunities for these types of interactions among colleagues:

- Conversations about their practice of teaching, including frank discussions about problems and sharing of possible solutions
- Observations of and evaluations about colleagues' teaching
- Collaborative design and evaluation of teaching materials
- Co-teaching and learning from each other

Special education teacher Therese Reder offers two examples of the many benefits of collaboration in action at Sussex Middle School in Wantage, NJ (personal communication, February 3, 2014):

Collaboration with my colleagues has helped me to grow into a stronger teacher of students with special needs. My colleague Rosemary Teufert has a great knowledge of technology and helped me with setting up a network of working iPads for our students who are nontraditional learners. This started out as a pilot program, but as time passed, Mrs. Teufert taught me many ways to enhance student learning through the use of technology. Students took to this approach and have learned to use the iPads and apps for all of their core subjects.

As a "seasoned" teacher, it is my pleasure to share my knowledge base and experience with new teachers. I love being a professional role model for them, but I also love that I, in turn, learn so much from them! These relationships help to keep my approach fresh and exciting as a teacher of middle school students, who often thirst for novelty. I am currently collaborating with a young teacher, Pam Saggau, who is giving me insightful new ideas on how to approach teaching *The Outsiders*.

School climate is also enhanced when the spirit of collaboration extends to administrator-teacher relationships. When teachers and principals partner to achieve common goals with a shared vision, "the paradigm shift will move toward parallel leadership in an environment in which educators learn to use their skills and expertise while working together to commit to taking on new leadership roles to facilitate school change and success" (Wilson & Conyers, 2010, p. 167).

AN END TO STRUGGLING IN ISOLATION

Making the most of social capital among educators in a school or district may require a fundamental shift in the way some teachers think about their work and in the scope of opportunities for collaboration provided to teachers. Allocating time and space for teachers to collaborate stands in opposition to the images that may flash through our brains as we think about our days in school and the traditional approach to teaching—"one of the loneliest professions," in the words of Hargreaves and Fullan (2012). Teachers spend most of their workdays alone in their classrooms, tackling complex and ever-changing challenges and confronting uncertainty without the benefit of consulting with their peers or receiving feedback and support.

In short, "uncertainty, isolation, and individualism are a toxic cocktail" (p. 107). By *individualism* the authors are not referring to *individuality*. They make the point that teachers must feel comfortable sharing their own views, even if they clash with those of the majority of their peers, and exhibiting their own unique personalities and outlooks. However, to return to the idea of collective efficacy, teachers should accept that working together with colleagues will produce gains in student learning and their own professional practice—and that every teacher can learn from and contribute to his or her fellow teachers.

Hargreaves and Fullan (2012) cite four factors that make it difficult for teachers to break out of this isolation:

Physical and metaphorical walls. In the architecture of traditional schools, teachers are assigned to separate classrooms or individual portable facilities with little or no time or space allotted for interacting with colleagues. This structure and schedule are the physical manifestations of habits and cultures that rely on and accept isolation as the way in which education must be provided.

The negative impact of teachers working without opportunities to interact and share with colleagues has long been identified as an impediment to significant educational reform. A classic sociological study by Lortie (1975) singled out isolation as one of the major obstacles to improving teaching practice and student achievement. Cohen and Spillane (1992) reported that this occupational seclusion is one reason for the "cluttered and fragmented accumulation of instructional guidance" (p. 41) that hampers attempts to institute more effective teaching approaches on a broad scale. Because teachers seldom gather to consult on their professional practice, "they receive fewer strong and consistent messages about content and pedagogy" (Berliner, 2009, p. 303).

Teachers agree with these educational researchers about the need for more time to work together. In a 2010 survey by Scholastic and the Gates Foundation, 89% of teachers ranked "more time to collaborate" as essential or very important to improving instruction and teacher retention. The same survey reported that teachers on average spend only 3% of the school day, about 15 minutes, interacting with their peers. "We need a better environment to share what works and what doesn't," said one survey respondent (p. 39).

Punishment vs. support. Evaluation systems based on pay and punishment may compel some teachers to seek out isolation as protection from what they view as negative scrutiny rather than supportive consultation. If teachers believe that sharing problems they have in their classrooms will be viewed as a sign of weakness in their practice, the result can be a self-perpetuating downward cycle of relying on ineffective strategies year after year. As one teacher noted, "It's dangerous to express vulnerability to experts or administrators because they will take your professional status away" (Leana, 2011, para. 4 under "Research Findings").

To reverse that cycle, teachers can benefit from opportunities to observe in each other's classrooms, to share challenges and ideas, and to reap constructive critiques from peer reviews. Teachers are much more likely to seek out information about their professional practice from their peers than from any other source—and to rank that input, feedback, and support as more relevant and useful. In a survey by the Center for Teaching Quality, more than two-thirds of teachers responding said other teachers were their primary sources of information about ways to improve their professional practice, more so than administrators, department chairs, and formal networks. In the teacher survey from Scholastic and the Gates Foundation (2010), 32% of respondents said peer reviews and observations would provide a "very accurate" assessment of their performance—a significantly higher rating than those of two other common performance measures, principal reviews (22%) and student grades and test scores (7%).

Tendency toward perfectionism. "Individualism can be a perverse product of teachers setting impossibly high expectations for themselves in a job with poorly defined limits" (Hargreaves & Fullan, 2012, p. 109). Effective teaching with the aim of helping all students realize more of their potential is not a sprint, or even a marathon. It is a continuous journey, day after day, year after year, in which performance is measured not in terms of perfection but by steady progress. It is easy for teachers to forget that in the seclusion of their classrooms.

When we make this point in workshops with teachers, many of them agree that the pursuit of perfection can stand in the way of progress. The paralyzing effect of refusing to complete a task and move on because there might be more we can do has a special hold on teachers who hear from politicians and some segments of the public that they can and should be doing more.

Pressure and time. To adapt an old saying, others may work from sun to sun, but a teacher's job is never done. Myriad roles and responsibilities are tied directly to teaching: preparing, delivering, and assessing the impact of lessons; guiding students' independent learning; interacting with students, parents, administrators, and support staff; and maintaining one's classroom. Add to that seemingly endless list tasks that don't help students learn or support the development of teachers' professional practice, such as additional paperwork and testing and hurried implementations of new curricular requirements and initiatives that may detract from rather than contribute to academic achievement. These additions to the to-do list create impossible time demands on teachers and may force them to retreat to the privacy of their classrooms to complete them. The weight of these tasks on top of the mentally and physically demanding work of teaching takes its toll on educators. As Haberman (1995) put it:

Life in the classroom does not occur in weeks, days, or even hours. It consists of intense periods of a few minutes, or even a few seconds, of endless interactions. To say that this is exhausting and draining is to refer to Niagara Falls as damp. (p. 71)

Haberman described the stamina necessary for teaching as evident in the enthusiasm good teachers exhibit for their work. "Stamina is a quality that is frequently taken for granted unless it is lacking" (p. 71). This fortitude is especially necessary for teachers of disadvantaged children whose families struggle in poverty, whose neighborhoods are marred by violence, who may not have the support they need to take on the hard work sometimes required for learning. This stamina is hard for teachers to maintain individually, but easier when they can share the load with colleagues. A school environment that facilitates collaboration and support among colleagues conveys the spirit of enthusiasm and high energy required for effective teaching. In some districts, teachers and administrators have worked together to revise school schedules, setting aside time for professional learning, collaboration, and implementation of new initiatives. Then the impact of those changes on student learning and instructional practice are assessed (Killion, 2013). Carving out time for purposeful collaboration among teachers is a hallmark of many high-performing education systems (see Chapter 6).

WHY AND HOW PURPOSEFUL COLLABORATION WORKS

There are many reasons why purposeful collaboration is so effective in supporting the development of teachers' professional practice and leadership abilities. Collaborative experiences can increase the joy in teaching, while reducing the isolation that may lead to increased frustration and stress. An aura of camaraderie is motivating and inspirational. Many teachers are more comfortable accepting input from colleagues who understand the challenges, pressures, and details of their work than from administrators. The give-and-take of contributing and receiving useful ideas and practical strategies is an efficient means of transferring and applying new information about teaching, and the combination of familiar and new perspectives sometimes facilitates seeing a problem from a different and illuminating angle. Teachers are more effective together than as individuals because they all have unique strengths, experiences, and perspectives to share.

Another reason that collaboration is so effective is that our brain chemistry is conducive to learning and working together. In *Social: Why Our*

Brains Are Wired to Connect (2013), Lieberman notes that rewards can be classified as either primary reinforcers, things that satisfy our basic needs (like food and water), or secondary reinforcers, things that are not initially rewarding but predict the presence or possibility of primary rewards. Money is the most common example of a secondary reinforcer: It can't keep you fed and warm, but it can buy food and heating fuel. Social regard or positive feedback from others is both a primary and a secondary reinforcer, because the brain's reward system is activated by praise from or positive interactions with other people. "Evolution built us to desire and work to secure positive social regard," Lieberman writes. "Why are we built this way? One possible explanation is that when humans . . . get together, work together, and care for one another, everyone wins" (p. 80).

Earlier in this chapter, we discussed trust as one of the essential elements in building social capital in groups. That sociological framework about the power of working together also has a biological basis. Researchers have found that the feeling of being trusted increases the release of oxytocin in the brain and bloodstream; the enhanced production of this neurochemical in turn may make people act in more trustworthy ways, creating what Zak (2012) calls a "virtuous cycle." Expert teachers who emphasize "building classroom community" at the start of each year recognize the centrality of this dynamic in their classrooms even if they have not been aware of the physiological mechanisms at work. Zak's studies, along with the work of Lieberman and other researchers, depict the brain as a "social organ," shaped by our need to connect with people and manage those interactions by interpreting and responding to the emotions of family, friends, colleagues, students, and others.

These findings call to mind the saying "They don't care how much you know until they know how much you care." These wise words are typically associated with working with students, but the same message can be applied to interacting with colleagues. Pamela Davidson, the mentor and resource teacher introduced earlier, also emphasizes the need to build relationships with colleagues as a foundation for sharing best practices.

Oxytocin plays a significant role in feelings of empathy and social attachment and affiliation, from the mother-infant bond at birth and onward in life. It is also tied to the production of dopamine, "a neurotransmitter that, when increased sufficiently, promotes feelings of pleasure, deep satisfaction, and motivation to repeat or continue the action that is associated with its release" (Willis, 2013, p. 122). The production of these neurochemicals and their impact on our social brains are being studied for possible applications in education, social learning, teamwork, and workplace collaboration (Lieberman, 2012; Zak, 2012). One implication of this research is the gains that may result in taking the time to build trust among colleagues working together to achieve shared goals, such as improving student learning.

WORKING TOGETHER TO IMPROVE COLLECTIVE PROFESSIONAL KNOWLEDGE

The importance of a trusting, caring school climate is reflected in the Teacher Leader Model Standards Domain I (Teacher Leadership Exploratory Consortium, n.d.):

> The teacher leader understands the principles of adult learning and knows how to develop a collaborative culture of collective responsibility in the school. The teacher leader uses this knowledge to promote an environment of collegiality, trust, and respect that focuses on continuous development in instruction and student learning.

We have seen the principles reflected in this standard at work in our interactions with teachers committed to collaborating for positive change in their schools and districts. In Donna's work as a school psychologist in Norman, OK, in the early 1990s, she worked with many educators who shared their time and expertise to serve on a task force dedicated to improving services for at-risk learners. The task force brought together regular and special education classroom teachers, school psychologists and counselors, administrators, and support staff. As a result of their collaborative research and planning, the district implemented:

- professional learning on a teaching approach to help learners develop cognitive and metacognitive skills that would help them progress across all core subjects;
- additional support for regular education teachers from special educators and school psychologists to meet the needs of at-risk learners in their classrooms; and
- more cohesive and systematic assessments and placements for students with learning challenges in middle and high school, including partnerships with community groups and employers for vocational training.

In this initiative and in Florida's STAR program (described in the Introduction), successful implementation relied on the active participation of teachers, on the recognition of the value of their professional perspectives and experiences, and on the development of opportunities for these teacher leaders to learn and share with their colleagues practical strategies that could be applied immediately in the classroom. In short, teachers can make a great difference in the lives of students when their wisdom and compassion are combined with better understanding of the science of learning and the strategies for helping all students to be successful. Professional learning communities provide an effective framework for facilitating these kinds of shared gains in knowledge and strategies.

Optimizing Opportunities in Professional Learning Communities

A study by University of North Carolina researchers (Moller et al., 2013) suggests that collective efficacy may be functioning at its best when school districts promote and establish policies and practices that (1) support teacher collaboration, in which teachers work together to increase student achievement, and (2) nurture professional communities in which teachers feel a sense of belonging and take pride in their school, understand the school's mission, and engage in ongoing professional development to learn new strategies to support student learning. Formal and informal learning communities can facilitate both aims.

Professional learning communities (PLCs) "are about people, practices, and processes—they are not a program. They are fundamentally a change in culture—the way we do work around here" (DuFour & Fullan, 2013, p. 16). PLCs are characterized by a shared mission, values, and goals, all focused on student learning; a collaborative culture; collective inquiry and an action orientation (also referred to as "learning by doing"); and a commitment to results through continuous improvement. "A collaborative culture and collective effort to support student and adult learning" are among the fundamental aspects of these professional communities (p. 14). DuFour and Fullan identify several ways that teacher collaboration can help bring about cultural changes that may be necessary to produce gains in student achievement:

- Amassing shared knowledge about why change is needed and how best to make it happen
- Enhancing collective capacity with the focus on improving student learning
- Sharing the results of change initiatives and using those results to inform and improve practice
- Nurturing a culture of collaboration and collective responsibility
- Establishing trust among colleagues and between administrators and teachers

Professional learning communities that have a lasting, positive impact on teachers' practice and on student achievement "require leadership that establishes a vision, creates opportunities and expectations for joint work, and finds the resources necessary to support the work, including expertise and time to meet" (Darling-Hammond, 2013, p. 106). The most successful PLCs facilitate positive and productive interactions among teachers engaged in collective inquiry and empowered to apply the results of those inquiries in their practice. When time is allotted for teachers to work together to plan lessons and provide instruction, to assess student progress, and to develop and plan how to deliver curriculum, "the benefits can include greater consistency in instruction, more willingness to share practices and try new ways of teaching, and more success in solving problems of practice" (p. 105).

Some schools and districts have found that an effective way to share best practices is through demonstrations by master teachers in model classrooms and informal or more formal peer evaluations based on class observations. "Perhaps the simplest way to break down professional isolation is for teachers to observe each other's teaching and to provide constructive feedback" (Darling-Hammond, 2013, p. 105).

Teacher Pam Saggau says she and colleagues at Sussex Middle School in Wantage, NJ, often collaborate by sharing lesson plans, ideas, projects, and websites, which "helps to keep things creative and fresh in the classrooms." These collaborations sometimes extend to teaching group lessons. "Students respond positively to these interactions and benefit from learning with different teachers and students," Saggau notes (personal communication, February 3, 2014).

Developing Your Skills as a Master Collaborator

We have established that there is a biological basis for affiliating with colleagues to work toward the achievement of shared goals, and that teachers working together are more effective than teachers working in isolation, due to the advantages of social capital. That does not mean that the ability to partner with colleagues comes naturally or easily to all teachers, but as with other skills in the teacher leadership tool kit, you can develop and strengthen your communication and teamwork acumen. Let's look at five areas where you can develop your skills to become a great collaborator:

1. A step-by-step process for working together to effect positive change

2. An understanding of how change reaches a "tipping point" for wide adoption
3. A communication approach to inspire (not require) teachers to work together
4. Tips for effective teamwork
5. Recommendations for mentoring new teachers

Working Together for Positive Change

It is difficult for one teacher working on his or her own to bring about significant change in a school or an educational system, but the collective efforts of committed educators can result in great strides toward improvements in student learning. Change is a process, not an event. The following example illustrates the change process step by step, along with key skills for change agents to develop:

Step 1: Establish Your Clear Intent. Let's say a group of 2nd- and 3rd-grade teachers are excited about applying what they've learned in a professional development workshop about using cognitive strategies to help children learn independently. The team decides to collaborate on lessons incorporating these strategies and on measuring their impact. These teachers will be more likely to succeed if they:

- Establish their motivation. The teachers should agree on the positive changes they expect to see from developing and implementing these lessons.
- Get ready by doing additional research—on the benefits of teaching students to "learn how to learn," on possible model lessons, and on likely outcomes they can use to measure their progress.
- Commit to the work that will be required for steady progress and ultimate success.

Step 2: Develop Your Action Plan. Proper planning and preparations are needed to turn intentions into actions. In our example, the teachers must agree on the metacognitive strategies that would be most appropriate and useful to introduce to their students, assign responsibilities for developing sample lessons, and determine timelines for completing the lessons and implementing them in classes. In his book *Changeology* (2012), Norcross advises, "Build your commitment and then make your goal public. Pick your start day and identify people who will support you. Take a few small initial steps—and prepare for liftoff!" (p. 83).

Step 3: Set Concrete Goals. Norcross uses the acronym SMART to advocate the development of goals for change that are specific, measurable, attainable, relevant, and time-specific. In our teacher workshops, we use the metaphor of a rocket launch to convey the importance of careful planning and goal setting in these early stages: The launch requires the most energy. If you commit the required resources, time, and effort to plan the launch, implementation will go much more smoothly.

In our continuing example, the teacher team developing lessons on the cognitive strategy of making comparisons devises sample lessons for use in math (comparing geometric shapes and properties), science (comparing animal attributes for classification), and social studies (comparing the holiday customs of students' family cultures). The team then creates rubrics to measure students' understanding of how comparisons can be useful and how well they use comparison to analyze lesson content. The team also sets benchmarks to guide teachers' assessments of whether the lessons have attained their goals. The sample lessons correspond to subjects scheduled to be taught in the coming weeks (relevance and timing).

Step 4: Take Action. Again, with full planning accomplished, implementation should be fairly straightforward. A small reward for the team may be in order to celebrate this milestone. For the team in our example, this reward takes the form of lunch at a local restaurant, where teachers take the time to compare notes on students' initial responses to learning about the use of cognitive strategies.

Step 5: Chart Course Corrections. Norcross (2012) refers to this stage as "managing slips." For nearly every implementation, the team is likely to encounter setbacks and unexpected occurrences. When these slips happen, the best approach is to persevere, to revisit the original planning and goals, and to identify necessary corrections to get back on track.

In the example of our teacher team implementing lessons on cognitive strategies, several teachers admitted they had not found time to continue introducing and offering practice with these skills, especially with preparation for standardized tests beginning. When other team members underscored the original intent of these lessons—to help children develop cognitive strategies they could use across core content and on these high-stakes tests—all the teachers pulled out their lesson plans and brainstormed ways to fit these lessons into core subjects and test preparation.

This is the stage where the cognitive asset we call *finishing power* (see Chapter 4) is most useful. Many projects are launched with great energy and enthusiasm but then get sidetracked by mistakes, difficulties, or the failure to complete all the necessary tasks. You may find the motivation to persist by looking on these setbacks as opportunities to learn and improve. It may also be helpful to call in reinforcements by asking supportive colleagues for their advice or input.

Step 6: Persist for Continued Progress. A common obstacle to long-term change is a dwindling commitment to the original goals or a tendency to turn to the "next big thing" and away from the need to maintain and continue to improve projects in process. As in the cognitive strategies team example, teachers need to persist in improving their initial lessons, adding new lessons and activities, and sharing the results with new teachers in their grades and with colleagues at other grade levels. Celebrations are also in order to emphasize both small and large gains resulting from the changes teams have produced.

One strategy that is useful in underscoring the need for persistence to accomplish a goal is a visual cue called a WinWeb (Wilson & Conyers, 2011a, pp. 268–269). WIN is an acronym for the question "What's Important Now?", a reminder to stay focused on key action steps and to celebrate progress through each of these steps. Around a big circle with several smaller circles inside of it, write the names of your most important projects in bubbles around the web. Chart progress toward achieving these projects, starting in the center with a dot along each web on the path to completion as you finish a path. This diagram supplies an informal, big-picture reminder of your progress and the need to keep working until you connect the dots. Many teachers tell us this strategy is useful both for their students and for keeping track of their own busy work and personal lives. The major advantages of the WinWeb process is that it:

- Keeps important goals front of mind. (In the daily rush of the small details of teaching, it is easy to overlook the big things.)
- Prompts thinking about key actionable steps.
- Makes it easier to keep track of a variety of priorities.
- Allows for celebrations of small wins over time.
- Is motivating to see progress and inspires that extra push to complete tasks.

Figure 3.1 offers an example of a WinWeb based on the steps and example of teacher collaboration set out in this section. To create a leadership WinWeb in collaboration with colleagues, adapt this diagram by following these steps:

1. Consider ideas from this book and other ideas that might help you achieve your leadership goals.

2. Choose which of these might be a priority for your team.
3. Identify action steps that would help you move toward your goals.
4. Label the key ideas you want to pursue.
5. Write in the action steps that might get you closer to achieving your goals.
6. Place a tick in the small circle as you complete an action step.
7. Track your progress over time.

Rogers's theory acknowledges that people go through these steps at widely varying speeds and in ways that influence how others around them respond to and adopt the innovation themselves. Some people are "innovators," the first in line to try out new things. Close behind them are "early adopters," who hear about a new idea and the positive responses of innovators about the benefits of adopting it. Following the early adopters in stages

Figure 3.1. Sample WinWeb on Working Together to Guide Students to Learn How to Learn Independently

are the early majority, the late majority, and the laggards; the latter may resist adopting a new idea until they are penalized in some way for resisting.

At the core of diffusion of innovations theory is the "tipping point" at which a new idea gains wider acceptance and adoption. The tipping point is the stage where small changes and advances have accumulated to gain significant momentum toward more profound progress. The question becomes, what can people who are in favor of this progress do to "move the dial" toward the tipping point? One of our goals in writing this book is to help move teacher leadership initiatives past the tipping point into the realm where teachers, administrators, and policymakers acknowledge their positive impact and agree on the need to integrate them into school systems.

In the school setting, the introduction and adoption of innovations take place within the social system of a collaborative work environment such as we've described in this chapter. Some strategies that might be useful in gaining support for positive change in your school or district include:

- Identifying and clearly communicating the benefits, repeatedly and by whatever means available, of adopting an innovation;
- Getting opinion leaders on your side, and seeking out the support of influential colleagues and administrators likely to become early adopters of an initiative and to spread the positive word to others;
- Marshalling organizational support by advocating for policy and procedural changes that will facilitate adoption of the innovation; and
- Taking advantage of social networks, electronic channels, and other engaging ways to make the case for change.

Communicating with Collaborators: Inspire, Don't Require

Making the case for positive change requires excellent communication skills, especially the ability to communicate respectfully and effectively with colleagues in a way that inspires cooperation and collaboration. Garmston (2013) suggests that a collaborative approach, characterized by social sensitivity and a willingness to take turns rather than dominate a discussion, will be more productive for teacher leaders in a group setting than a take-charge assertiveness.

In most school cultures, teachers work together as equals. Thus, even those in positions of implied or expressed authority would do well to communicate in a way that acknowledges that all teachers contribute to the school's culture and its central mission to support student learning. As Kouzes and Posner (2012) advise, "You can't command commitment;

you have to inspire it. You have to enlist others in a common vision by appealing to shared aspirations." (p. 18). To better ensure that your colleagues will understand and accept the benefits of adopting new effective teaching practices, working and learning together in PLCs, and embracing leadership opportunities on their own, seek to inspire, not require, their active participation. Effective communications among colleagues adhere to these standards:

- **Attentive listening.** When you convey that you value your coworkers' contributions, you exhibit the foremost sign of respect.
- **Empathy and understanding.** Take the time to understand colleagues' needs, aspirations, and points of view.
- **Unity of purpose.** The point at which interests intersect is the starting point for successful collaboration.
- **Credibility.** People will be more likely to heed your suggestions for action if they know you are a person who does what you say you will do. To build trust, ensure that your actions as a teacher and colleague are consistent with your stated words. If you say you will do something, do it. Follow through, and follow up.
- **Willingness to consider new ideas.** Innovative ideas are more likely to be shared in an open atmosphere where colleagues feel comfortable introducing new teaching strategies and approaches without fear that they will be disparaged or ignored. Instead of pointing out immediately why an idea probably won't work, consider affirming a colleague's contribution and adding to it. This "Yes, and . . . " approach is at the core of improvisational comedy at The Second City, but it has also been applied successfully in workplaces to enhance teamwork, collaboration, and a shared innovative mindset (Leonard & Yorton, 2015).

Optimize Your Teams

A classic article from the *Harvard Business Review* (Katzenbach & Smith, 2005) sums up six key pointers to make work teams as effective as possible:

1. Keep the team as small as possible to get the job done. Katzenbach and Smith note that most of the effective teams they studied had 10 or fewer members. In a school setting, four to eight people work together well. If your list of team members includes a dozen or more colleagues, you might consider splitting responsibilities among smaller teams.
2. Bring together team members with complementary skills.

3. Identify your common purpose. "Teams develop direction, momentum, and commitment by working to shape a meaningful purpose" (p. 3).
4. Set specific performance goals.
5. Share the work by making concrete assignments of responsibility, and share the leadership.
6. Establish mutual accountability. "No group ever becomes a team until it can hold itself accountable as a team. . . . Team accountability is about the sincere promises we make to ourselves and others, promises that underpin two critical aspects of effective teams: commitment and trust" (p. 6).

Workplace studies on the habits of "star performers" find that these employees do more than just "their part" on a team: They encourage fellow team members to contribute to setting goals, assigning work tasks, and establishing timelines. In effect, they facilitate a synchronized flow of ideas with everyone's input and buy-in, which in turn fosters a more positive and productive environment (Pentland, 2014).

This advice from the business world echoes recommendations from DuFour and Fullan (2013) about teams working in professional learning communities: "Meaningful collaborative teams benefit from common goals that are immediately applicable to their schools and classrooms. They also benefit from shared responsibility for engaging in collective inquiry specifically designed to improve instructional practice and student learning" (p. 68).

Putting Collaboration Skills to Work Mentoring New Colleagues

A common form of collaboration is mentoring in new teacher induction programs. Because these teachers are just beginning their careers in education, they typically need more than a "buddy" or a "local guide" to show them around the school and its policies and procedures. New teachers benefit from the guidance of "situated" or "educative" mentoring provided by "teachers of teachers," to use a title suggested by Norman & Feiman-Nemser (2012). Mentors of new teachers are expected "to contribute to new teachers' learning and to influence the quality of their teaching" and to enable "new teachers to do with some help what they were not ready to do on their own" (p. 302).

Educative mentoring may take the form of guiding new teachers to reflect on their practice—on how teaching differs from their expectations based on their teacher education and student teaching, on what works and doesn't seem to work in their classroom, on why some approaches are more effective than others, and on what they might do differently. This guidance might be more direct, as in co-teachers, or mentors working alongside new teachers to accomplish challenging aspects of teaching. In either approach, strong mentors are skillful observers, careful listeners, and able demonstrators, with an extensive "vocabulary of learning" to model and explain useful strategies and approaches.

In today's classrooms, where diverse students represent a wide range of current levels of ability and understanding, new teachers may need guidance not just in the basic components of the job of teaching, like classroom management, but also in taking a wider view of what is happening in the minds of students and how teachers can most effectively guide each student to learn. This may be a broader concept of mentoring than the standard approach, encompassing both new understandings about how the brain learns and classic views put forth by Dewey that teachers must be curious about what is happening in the minds of their students and what that means for how they teach them (Feiman-Nemser, 2012).

Mentoring new teachers is most effective when it is integrated into a school culture "organized to benefit both the novice and the experienced teachers, and structures are in place that further facilitate teacher interaction and reinforce interdependence" (Johnson et al., 2004, p. 159). This type of culture recognizes the positive dynamics when new and veteran teachers interact as colleagues, sharing ideas and working together to plan lessons and activities, strengthen formative assessments, and implement new initiatives and learning tools. It prizes mentoring as a source of support for new teachers and an avenue of renewal for their colleagues.

CONSTRUCTIVE CONCLUSIONS: THE POWER OF OPTIMIZING OPPORTUNITIES FOR PURPOSEFUL COLLABORATION

This chapter discussed research on the gains that can be made when teachers work together for positive change in their schools and districts. As Kouzes and Posner (2012) note, professional challenges "tend to bring out the best in people. . . . Meeting new challenges always requires things to be different than they currently are. You can't respond with the same old solutions. You have to change the status quo" (p. 159). By taking advantage of and advocating for opportunities to collaborate, teachers can better take on the challenges facing their profession.

Purposeful collaboration elevates professional practice, turning good teachers into great teachers by enhancing the collective efficacy and collective intelligence of all educators in a school or district. Formal and informal professional learning communities offer opportunities for teachers to learn together, plan together, conduct action research, implement new initiatives, provide support and constructive feedback through peer observations, and share ideas and information. This chapter offered several recommendations for building your communication, collaboration, and teamwork skills and for applying research on implementing innovative teaching approaches. These parting suggestions offer further support for the power of collaboration.

Be an active participant. Some teachers are "joiners" and others are not, but everyone has something to gain and contribute by working together to improve student learning. Taking advantage of opportunities to share ideas, ask for suggestions, lend support, and sometimes just offer an empathetic ear to help break down the walls of isolation and build professional and social capital in their place.

Take advantage of your profession's embrace of lifelong learning. You have much to contribute based on your education and professional experiences—and much to gain in learning from the ideas and suggestions of colleagues. When fellow teachers share a problem or seek advice, there is no question about competence, only acceptance that you are all working together to improve teaching in your school. Along the same lines, sharing ideas and successes is not dismissed as bragging but welcomed as a contribution to collective efficacy. And remember: Lifelong learning helps to maintain brainpower.

Learn to listen and ask. As in all forms of community, diplomacy and empathy are useful skills for teachers to develop as they work together to optimize student learning. Continue to develop the delicate art of listening carefully to the questions and frustrations shared by colleagues. Ask "Have you thought about this?" "Have you tried this?" "May I suggest this?" "May I come in and share something that has worked for me?"

Take the initiative. Look for ways to enhance collaboration, camaraderie, and shared learning among your colleagues. Tammy Daugherty's "Breakfast with the Brain" presentations to colleagues and the book study group organized by Theresa Dodge (see Chapter 1) are two examples of shared learning and purposeful collaboration.

CHAPTER 4

Work Smarter

Metacognition and Developing Expertise

The knack for reflecting on our own thoughts is often viewed as a hallmark of the human mind. It is also a vital survival skill.

—Stephen M. Fleming, 2014

Applying the Pareto Principle, which holds that 80% of output derives from 20% of input, to education suggests that student achievement might be enhanced by wielding a small number of teaching and learning strategies that can generate significant results. Teacher leadership and purposeful collaboration are among the 20% of endeavors educators can undertake to optimize student learning—and metacognition improves classroom instruction as well as leadership activities and interactions with colleagues, administrators, parents, and other educational stakeholders. This chapter presents the third component of the POWER framework for teacher leadership, exploring how you can work smarter by becoming more metacognitive in your professional practice and leadership and collaborative roles.

That's not to say there are shortcuts to becoming a great teacher and teacher leader. Like any worthwhile undertaking, improving teaching practice and collaborating with colleagues intent on the same goal are ongoing endeavors that span a career. Teaching is among the most complex of professions. Each fall, a teacher begins the school year with a new group of students, each of them unique in their blend of learning strengths, challenges, interests, personality, and existing knowledge and experiences. Every day requires preparation to take on new and unexpected opportunities and quandaries. The profession requires teachers to educate, communicate, motivate, demonstrate, investigate, negotiate, orchestrate, and celebrate; to empathize and organize; to listen, lead, follow, guide, encourage, and learn alongside students and colleagues.

Great teachers and great teacher leaders do not owe their effectiveness to innate "gifts," but rather to their hard work and commitment. They must continually hone their knowledge and skills to focus their unique blend of strengths and abilities. Florida State University professor K. Anders Ericsson has written extensively about the development of expertise as the product of sustained effort, self-assessment, and deliberate practice. In fields as diverse as chess, music, and medicine, the common denominator among outstanding performers is their willingness to devote a decade or more—in the range of 10,000 hours of learning, practice, coaching, and thinking about how to improve execution of tasks beyond their current levels of competence and comfort (Ericsson, Prietula, & Cokely, 2007).

The concept of deliberate practice is similar to the adherence at the organizational level to continual improvement in the business sector and definitely applies to developing your expertise as an educator and teacher leader: Over time, through repeated execution of the tasks of teaching followed by rigorous assessment and re-evaluation for potential improvements, your work becomes more effective and efficient. But you are always on the lookout for new strategies, continually analyzing what works and what doesn't, and sharing and comparing notes with colleagues on new ideas and possible solutions to persistent challenges.

METACOGNITION IN SUPPORT OF DEVELOPING ADAPTIVE EXPERTISE

Metacognition is an essential tool in the development of expertise as a teacher and teacher leader. In fact, "metacognition may be seen as a foundation for learning, achievement, and success in almost any field" (Fleming, 2014). *Metacognition* can be defined as "thinking about thinking" and "knowing about knowing." Teachers who use metacognition are aware of and have control over the way they think about their teaching. This awareness and control takes the form of effectively planning, implementing, and evaluating their teaching practice. Metacognitive educators adjust their teaching strategies and approach based on their assessment of the needs of their students, their own intentionality, and the context of the lesson and subject matter (Hartman, 2002). As a result, teachers who use metacognition are likely to perceive themselves as having greater efficacy than those who do not.

This form of self-reflection and self-assessment can also enhance the leader's contributions to the professional community through purposeful collaboration and teacher leadership. Developing adaptive expertise so that you are prepared to add to your base of professional knowledge and skills throughout your career entails being able to think metacognitively about your teaching practice and about how you learn and collaborate with colleagues and administrators (Bransford, Darling-Hammond, & LePage, 2005; Hatano & Inagaki, 1986). Metacognition can help each of us understand our unique contribution to our profession.

The good news for teacher leaders is that you can train your brain to become more metacognitive about your professional practice. And as with other forms of learning, developing metacognition may actually change your brain. Neuroscientist Stephen Fleming (2014) and a team of researchers at University College London found that subjects who demonstrated metacognition at higher levels than other study participants had more gray matter in the anterior prefrontal cortex and more white matter (which aids in transmitting electrical impulses from neuron to neuron) connecting the anterior prefrontal cortex to other parts of the brain. Neuroscientists continue to study how the brain supports metacognition and whether and how this research might lead to discoveries of ways to enhance metacognition.

Today when a busy teacher is expected to do even more with less, using metacognitive strategies can make a great difference in the effectiveness of an educator and teacher leader. Such a leader can guide colleagues in learning to work smarter by applying cognitive and metacognitive strategies to leadership and collaboration activities. In professional practice, this approach takes the form of (1) professional learning and self-reflection on ongoing efforts to improve what works in the classroom and (2) collaborating with colleagues and advocating for resources and support. Teacher leaders can model and help connect their colleagues to research and resources about the value of a metacognitive approach to teaching, learning, and leading.

A wide body of research demonstrates the positive impact on academic achievement of teaching students cognitive and metacognitive strategies that allow them to become self-directed learners (Bransford et al., 2000; Hattie, 2009; Wang, Haertel, & Walberg, 1993). In fact, analyzing a summary of studies of different-aged learners performing various tasks in different domains, Veenman (2011) estimated that students' skillfulness at using metacognition accounts for 40% of the variance in learning outcomes. Teachers who have studied with us say they enjoy learning how to use metacognition in their teaching practice—and in their lives—as a tool to become functionally smarter while simultaneously guiding students to become what we call the "boss of their brains."

However, "despite the recognition of the role of metacognition in student success, limited research has been done to explore teachers' explicit awareness of their metacognition and their ability to think about, talk about, and write about their thinking" (Wilson & Bai, 2010). Metacognitive teaching involves the use of two types of metacognition: strategic knowledge and executive management strategies. Students can be taught *strategic knowledge*, or how, when, and why to use a toolbox of effective higher-order thinking skills. They can also learn *executive management strategies* to monitor the effectiveness of using cognitive skills and their learning. Teachers also employ executive management strategies to metacognitively plan, monitor, and evaluate their lessons and units and to reflect on their practice.

Teaching often involves complex decisionmaking minute by minute in order to guide students in achieving their learning goals. Effective teachers know there is no autopilot in education: Given the complexities of managing the learning and behaviors of a room full of diverse learners, teachers must make more than 1,000 decisions each school day (Kauchak & Eggen, 2013). Effective teachers think about and regulate instruction at all three phases of teaching: planning (before), monitoring (during), and evaluation (after). By using a metacognitive process employing the strategies we outline in this chapter, teachers can optimistically and intentionally plan, monitor, and evaluate their teaching practice and enhance their collaborative interactions in professional communities.

Self-reflection on one's practice and values as a teacher is a key element of deep learning, which has been described as "an action research approach to professional development" in which educators "are conscious of what they are doing, why they are doing it—and ask themselves questions about the actions that they take and the decisions that they make" (Stoll, McKay, Kember, Cochoran-Smith, & Lytle, 1997). A metacognitive approach to teaching and leading enhances both daily practice and contributions to high-level school reform, as Kennedy suggests: Teachers' "thoughts interact with their actions every day in both large and small ways, influencing their responses to new policies, new curricula, and new ideas about practice as they arise" (2008, p. 21).

LEADING WITH METACOGNITION

In a 1991 analysis that remains relevant to our discussions about teacher leadership today, Susan Rosenholtz identified two distinctive types of school cultures: *stuck* and *moving*. In schools stuck with lower levels of academic achievement, educators regard teaching as technically easy, usually work in isolation in their classrooms, and seldom seek out help and feedback. In moving schools, by comparison, teachers understand that their profession is a complex and difficult endeavor; they consistently seek out help and opportunities to collaborate with colleagues and, as a result, their teaching practice continuously improves. Teachers in moving schools recognize that learning how to teach more effectively is an ongoing process. Support from colleagues leads these teachers to have a higher level of confidence and certainty about achieving their goals and about optimal ways of achieving them. "It is assumed that improvement in teaching is a collective rather than individual enterprise and that analysis, evaluation, and experimentation in concert with colleagues are conditions under which conditions improve" (p. 73).

When educators have opportunities to work together to improve their teaching practice and reflect on what works and what doesn't in the classroom, they develop higher degrees of both individual and collective efficacy (Goddard & Goddard, 2001). This shared perception that teachers are equipped with and committed to using effective teaching techniques is "systematically associated with student achievement" (Goddard, Hoy, & Hoy, 2000, p. 480). Therefore, teachers applying a metacognitive approach both to their practice and to purposeful collaboration with colleagues and administrators directly supports student learning.

Metacognitive teachers also are able to assume one of the most important roles of teacher leaders—that is, the role of learner (Harrison & Killion, 2007). As learners, teachers demonstrate lifelong learning, model continuous learning, and apply what they learn to help all students and their colleagues succeed. In faculty meetings and professional development these expert learners are willing to try new strategies, and their enthusiasm is contagious.

According to TLMS Domain III: "The teacher leader understands the evolving nature of teaching and learning, established and emerging technologies, and the school community. The teacher leader uses this knowledge to promote, design, and facilitate job-embedded professional learning aligned with school improvement goals." A metacognitive approach to teaching, leading, and purposeful collaboration can help you attain this standard of teacher leadership.

SIX COGNITIVE ASSETS FOR METACOGNITIVE TEACHING AND LEADERSHIP

To thrive amid "the enormous amount of ambiguity, unpredictability, and occasional chaos" of life in the classroom (Jackson, 1990, p. 149), teachers must be continually and actively engaged in the wide range of tasks involved in guiding students' learning. Initiatives such as the Common Core State Standards aim to improve student achievement, but they also add to the demands on teachers; additional layers of curricular requirements and standards may make it more difficult to stay focused on what really matters in the long term—learning content and goals.

It's tempting to think that the intricacies of teaching can be simplified by relying on standard procedures, but "teaching is not a line of work that can be reduced to a set of skills or that can be prescribed from afar; instead, it should be viewed as professional work that requires thought, judgment, and knowledge" (Kennedy, 2008, p. 23). The following six-part model on metacognitive teaching and leading is adapted from our *Thinking for Results* approach to teaching (Wilson & Conyers, 2011b), which makes use of vital cognitive assets for thinking and learning. These principles for metacognitive teaching can be applied across various content domains, contexts for teaching, and roles for purposeful collaboration and leadership. All adult learners are not "naturally metacognitive," but can learn to wield self-reflective tools and strategies to improve professional practice (and, as an added bonus, personal pursuits as well). In addition, a leader can use these same tools to develop a "synergy of strengths" in the school and district by supporting colleagues to identify, enhance, and apply their practical, creative, and organizational strengths.

Cognitive Asset 1: Clear Intent

We touched briefly in Chapter 3 on the need to establish and maintain common goals to optimize teamwork. Here we revisit and expand on the concept of developing your clear intent in both classroom practice and in coaching, mentoring, and collaborating with colleagues. Clear intent involves sustaining a well-defined sense of what your intentions are in the classroom and in interactions with students, fellow teachers, administrators, parents, and other educational stakeholders. Maintaining your clear intent enhances the likelihood of attaining what you set out to do. For example, teachers who have "the clear intention of increasing student learning by constantly improving their instructional skills will tend to increase their effectiveness and achieve their goals" (Wilson & Conyers, 2011b, p. 145).

In short, establishing clear intent helps a teacher leader stay focused on what really matters. Applied to classroom practice, clear intent becomes the touchstone for the ultimate goal of increasing student learning. Without it, it's easier to get sidetracked by an emphasis on planning and monitoring procedures and activities (e.g., Are students following the steps for this activity correctly? Did students comply with the time requirements for their presentations? Did they cite at least a minimum number of sources in their papers?). Meanwhile a teacher can lose sight of the most fundamental question: Is each student learning? That's not to say procedures and activities don't matter. They do. But the ultimate measure of their effectiveness is in learning outcomes. In that cliché about not being able to see the forest for the trees, lesson plans and classroom procedures are the trees, but the real goal is a thriving forest of student achievement.

Optimizing clear intent in the classroom extends to sharing your intent and learning objectives with students. Oftentimes, teachers are so keen to get into a lesson that they may not share its objectives.

Along the same lines, establishing clear intent can help optimize teacher collaboration and leadership endeavors. When mentoring a new colleague, for example, it is helpful for mentor and novice to talk through the most crucial intentions of their interactions. Certainly, the mentor wants to build trust, to share ideas, and to offer support, but at its core, the mentoring relationship is about improving classroom practice. When creating a presentation for a professional development workshop, the clear intent might be to explain and demonstrate an instructional strategy that colleagues can apply immediately in their classrooms.

Thus, clear intent helps establish a firm foundation for a metacognitive approach to teaching and leading. This is precisely why metacognition should be front and center in preservice and inservice programs. Expectations are high for teachers to increase students' academic performance and personal and social development amid continual changes in national, state, and district standards (Ingersol, 2005; Smylie, Miller, & Westbrook, 2008). Educators need to be able to collaborate in purposeful, intentional groups to apply these sometimes vague and even contradictory standards so they can best meet student needs in the context of their current levels of performance. Discussions about intentionality are most productive when teachers can collaborate both across and within grade levels. The majority of joint planning on lessons, units, and curriculum should occur within grade level groups, but without vertical planning, learning outcomes may lack coherence as students progress from grade to grade.

As general studies principal at Rohr Middle School in North Miami Beach, FL, Staci Berry views one aspect of her clear intent as sharing and modeling teaching strategies that have been shown to be effective in classrooms of diverse learners. "I try to model different modes of instruction—less teacher talk and more visuals and kinesthetic learning," Berry says. "I see in the middle school what a difference it makes when you get off the stage and facilitate more social learning. That's how I've modeled it, and it's really taken off." School administrators should seek to support "learning communities that foster teamwork, social learning, and the sharing of best practices, which are critical for all accomplished teachers," Berry adds (personal communications, January 23, 2015).

GUIDING QUESTIONS ON CLEAR INTENT

- What key knowledge and experiences do we want our students to have?
- How can we best ensure that this happens?

Cognitive Asset 2: Systematic Planning

Following on the heels of establishing a clear intent comes a metacognitive approach to planning. This approach extends beyond traditional lesson planning to keep the focus on purposeful learning goals—not just the sequence of activities in a lesson but what students are expected to learn, how to enhance the likelihood that the diverse learners in the class will learn it, and how to evaluate how successfully they have learned the lesson content.

In this aspect of metacognitive teaching, group planning and collaboration can help keep the focus on learning goals and objectives; on identifying and addressing students' prior knowledge and likely preconceptions; on gathering, selecting, and sequencing useful instructional strategies; and on recognizing and preparing for potential learning obstacles. Collaborative planning may guide thinking about lesson content, teaching strategies, and students' learning in different ways and may offer new ideas and perspectives. A 1st-grade teacher offers this view of the range of discussions that take place when colleagues share their instruction planning and clear intent:

> We talk about lesson-planning activities we're going to do, about how activities went, and things that we had planned to do. . . . We talk about testing. We talk about students and different problems they might have, trying to come up with solutions for them. (Conley & Muncey, 2011, p. 134)

A vital aspect of brain-based teaching, which can be defined as the optimization of student-centered instruction, is considering how students' prior knowledge and experiences may influence their learning:

> There is a good deal of evidence that learning is enhanced when teachers pay attention to the knowledge and beliefs that learners bring to a learning

task, use this knowledge as a starting point for new instruction, and monitor students' changing conceptions as instruction proceeds. (Bransford et al., 2000, p. 11)

By identifying what students know and what they think they know, a teacher can better plan learning activities that build on existing knowledge and help to set aside faulty assumptions. Planning so that students have interesting problems to solve and providing background information they may lack are key to fostering an engaging learning environment.

Just as developing capability to understand students' current points of view can enhance student learning, honing the ability to consider the perspectives and experiences of colleagues and administrators can provide a useful resource on effective teaching strategies. In addition, recognizing and respecting others' points of view facilitates open dialogue among colleagues by valuing everyone's contributions in team meetings and school improvement efforts. At the same time, leaders reflect on how their own prior knowledge, experiences, values, and assumptions guide interactions and responses to others' perspectives and contributions.

Applying metacognition to the gathering, selection, and sequencing of instructional strategies is another component of this approach to planning. Because each brain is unique and students learn through different pathways (Berninger & Richards, 2002), presenting new information in a variety of formats and learning activities is more likely to engage more students and enhance their learning. Christenbury (2010/2011) suggests that varying instruction based on students' needs and preferences is a hallmark of high-quality teaching: "Effective teachers use a variety of strategies and a range of methods, and they change and refine these over time. They do not teach the same way and use the same instructional repertoire year after year." In the quest to expand one's teaching tool kit of instructional strategies, colleagues near and far are robust sources of new strategies and ideas. From team meetings to online forums like Edutopia, both teachers and students can benefit from the wealth of lesson content and instructional strategies that have been successful in the classrooms of other educators. Emerging as well as experienced teacher leaders can share their own effective strategies at these sites. This valuable exchange of ideas exemplifies engaging in and sharing research to enhance pedagogy from our spectrum of teacher leadership opportunities (Chapter 1).

A final example of employing metacognition in planning is in anticipating student learning challenges. In the course of a lesson, various types of misconceptions can occur, related both to content (e.g., understanding the implications of historical events) and process (e.g., systematically planning how to solve a math problem). Planning how to head off or respond to these challenges is another area where collaborating with colleagues may be extremely useful. What has proven to be difficult for students in other classrooms to understand and apply when this content was taught? What were some of the ways other teachers sought to overcome these challenges, and which strategies worked best? Expert teachers know that often certain aspects of a lesson are likely to trip up some or all of their students; in team meetings and other opportunities for collaboration, they can share how to introduce the lesson to decrease the likelihood of learning problems, how to spot and address problems with comprehension during the lesson, and how to evaluate learning outcomes and identify any need for additional instructional assistance. In keeping with the support for new teachers component of the leadership spectrum, this type of sharing may be especially useful for teachers just beginning their careers in the classroom, who do not have the same level of experience as their more veteran colleagues in spotting and responding to learning challenges.

In sum, collaboration is an effective means of weaving metacognition into instructional planning. In an example from an Oklahoma school district in which many 2nd graders had learning challenges, Donna, a school psychologist, partnered with three teachers at one elementary school to teach the students metacognitive and cognitive strategies for learning. Not only did the students have content gaps in their prior knowledge, but they also had gaps in their knowledge of how to learn. Through this collaborative effort—with the expertise in teaching and modeling cognitive strategies needed for learning provided by the school psychologist and the 2nd-grade teachers contributing their content expertise—the team was able to teach in ways that produced results by the end of the school year. Assessments revealed gains in content knowledge and the students' ability to employ and benefit from the use of metacognitive strategies and cognitive assets. By pooling individual professional strengths, this team approach lightened the load for everyone and distributed the benefits of this shared expertise to students in all three classrooms.

GUIDING QUESTIONS ON SYSTEMATIC PLANNING

- What challenges might students encounter with this lesson?
- How can we plan our lessons and instructional strategies to ensure we meet our students' learning needs?

> • Who among our colleagues has taught this lesson successfully, and what might we learn from them?

Cognitive Asset 3: Monitoring

Professional conversations, mentoring, and coaching are also a big part of enhancing your use of the third strategy in a metacognitive approach to teaching and leadership—that is, monitoring student learning with an emphasis on recognizing when the need arises to reteach, offer additional instructional support, or try different strategies. As Kennedy reports:

> When making specific decisions, teachers rarely consider alternative courses of action, and when they do, they don't consider very many alternatives. Once teachers are engaged in their lessons, roughly 40%–50% of all teachers' thoughts during instruction have to do with students—what they are learning or what they are doing. Goals and content comprised only 5% or less of all thoughts, and instructional procedures comprised 20%–30% of their thoughts. (2008, p. 23)

According to standards formulated by the National Council of Teachers of English (2013), monitoring students' performance *during* learning, not just after lessons and units are complete, embodies formative assessment. This metacognitive approach to monitoring academic performance:

- • stays focused on individual students' needs and progress;
- • provides immediate, actionable feedback to facilitate the most productive next steps toward learning success;
- • emphasizes progress and growth;
- • reflects the goals and intentions of both students and their teacher; and
- • engages students in taking charge of their learning.

Formative assessment recognizes the "contextual" characteristic of effective teaching and the need to "alter, adjust, and change instruction depending on who is in the classroom and the extent to which those students are achieving" (Christenbury, 2010/2011). The gains that are possible when teachers and students purposefully and continually monitor learning progress spans all grade levels and even applies to adult learning, as these examples demonstrate:

- Periodic progress monitoring of the range of skills students are expected to develop over the course of the school term (as opposed to just the knowledge and skills taught in a specific lesson or unit) offers several benefits: "students learn more, teacher decisionmaking improves, and students become more aware of their own performance" (Safer & Fleischman, 2005). In an example of using "probes" (brief, easily administered measures of the range of skills taught in a core subject) weekly to assess 3rd-graders' developing reading skills, Safer and Fleischman note that teachers can more effectively adjust instructional intensity guided by these regular progress checks. They can slow down and provide additional instruction and time for practice or step up to the next level of textual complexity. In addition, students are motivated to "make the line go up" as they chart their weekly results.

- Motivating students to take charge of their learning may present a challenge even at the high school and college level. In teaching a writing course, Christenbury (2010/2011) relates how she needed to set clear expectations for academic conduct, ramp up instructional intensity, and make writing assignments more relevant to their needs to engage the intellectual curiosity of her students after determining early in the term that they "were not prepared for the requirements of the course as I had designed it." She further involved students by asking for their feedback on course requirements and, based on their advice, gave them more time for assignments and more feedback on their writing drafts. This example demonstrates the need for continual monitoring and flexibility to adapt teaching techniques to meet students' needs.

- When teachers have opportunities to co-teach and to learn and teach together, these collaborations help us to see more clearly what is happening with students—as when one teacher is observing as a colleague teaches, for example.

To emphasize knowledge gains in professional development with colleagues, we suggest the "group aloud summary," which teachers at our workshops have enjoyed. At the end of each day, we ask participants to stand up and answer in unison questions about the content and process of that session. This can be a bit cacophonous, but it also assists learners in recognizing the vast amount of information they and their colleagues have learned and experiences they have had in one day.

Carefully planning instruction is crucial to effective teaching, but so is the willingness to be flexible and change course when monitoring students' progress indicates that it is necessary to do so. Even when you have given thought to students' needs and anticipated their challenges during planning, once the lesson begins and you observe your students' responses and performance, you may well contemplate a course correction with the pace of sharing new information, the sequence and timing of the lesson, the methods for teaching, or all the above.

Kelly Rose, EdD, a library media specialist in Florida, shares a simple example of monitoring student comprehension in framing a technology lesson: In planning the lesson, she and a classroom teacher, who were co-teaching the unit, decided to begin with the question: "What is a good use of Google Drive?" But when they posed that question to students, the response was silence and blank faces. Rather than moving on immediately to the lesson content, they tried again with a different question to gauge students' existing knowledge, "How can we use Google Drive?" There was still no response. So the teachers posed the question in a slightly different way: "How can Google Drive help us?" "As a broader question, the students were able to access more information and could converse about their Internet use for gathering information," Rose reports. Learning together helped us as educational professionals to carefully observe and shift in real time so as to ensure students understood what we were asking" (personal correspondence, November 11, 2014).

GUIDING QUESTIONS ON MONITORING

- How is my teaching proceeding?
- Are students learning as planned?
- How might I need to change my plan to ensure students learn at high levels?

Cognitive Asset 4: Evaluation

Hand in hand with planning and monitoring comes a metacognitive approach to evaluation, in assessing the extent to which learning objectives are achieved and in measuring teaching effectiveness. As with formative assessments in the monitoring phase, constructive evaluations encompass gains and gaps both in student learning and instructional techniques and strategies. Assessment of teaching performance requires that we use *appropriate courage* to examine potential areas for improving our professional practice. Appropriate courage "involves accurately assessing a situation and the inherent risks, being clear on mission and goals, deciding what action to take, and being clear about what resources are needed and what an appropriate timeline is" (Wilson & Conyers, 2011b, p. 224). Applying this cognitive asset to evaluating our practice, teachers can work together to become more open to suggestions and recommendations from colleagues and administrators to enhance our instructional approach. As discussed in Chapter 2, teaching has long been an isolated profession; however, 21st-century education demands that classroom doors be flung open and that teachers be able to rely on their peers for observations, advice, and ideas for improvement in the complex endeavor of teaching a roomful of unique brains. Thus, teachers must have the courage to acknowledge possible shortcomings so that they can benefit from the collective expertise of their professional community.

There is likely room for improvement in all classrooms when it comes to implementing new curricular requirements and standards. Due to the attentional requirements involved in mastering new instructional content and strategies, all teachers go through periods of clumsiness when we are learning something new. We can do ourselves a favor by recognizing that evaluating new lessons carefully will allow us to pinpoint what worked and what didn't and to use these assessments to improve our future delivery. Being able to rely on mentoring, teacher learning groups, and learning partners can be particularly important during these periods. Instead of settling on a self-inflicted verdict that "I'm just not good at teaching this," we can look for ways to hone our practice and aim for steady incremental gains.

In our Thinking for Results approach, we call this commitment to persist in spite of difficulties to complete important tasks *finishing power*. Strategies in support of enhancing finishing power include identifying your priorities (the most important steps on the way to achieving your goals), tracking your progress in working through each of those steps, and celebrating when you accomplish what you have set out to do. In the case of implementing new lessons, for example, your priorities may be to:

1. develop and carry out the new unit;
2. identify how you will monitor the lesson in progress and evaluate its effectiveness at its completion;
3. share results with colleagues and seek ideas for improvements from your collective experiences; and
4. implement those improvements the next time around.

Thus, this formulation of finishing power does not end after the first time you deliver a new lesson. Instead, it encompasses the stage of evaluation, self-reflection, and sharing with colleagues as a pathway to continually improving one's practice.

GUIDING QUESTIONS ON EVALUATION

- To what degree were learning objectives reached?
- Do we need to change the way we monitor and assess effectiveness?

Cognitive Asset 5: Learning from Experience

Closely connected to the metacognitive and cognitive strategies that support the monitoring and evaluation phases is an ongoing commitment to learning from experience, both individual experiences and the shared wisdom of the professional community. Life in the classroom provides myriad opportunities to learn from experience. No matter how many years you have been teaching, the new students who enter your classroom every term make every day and every lesson different than the last time around. You can and should apply your previous experiences, but at the same time stay alert to the need to adjust your lessons and instructional approach to the unique needs and strengths of the students before you. The overarching resource for learning from experience is metacognition—that is, thinking about our thoughts and actions with a mind toward change when it is necessary.

Wise teachers:

- make it a habit to evaluate learning outcomes and instructional effectiveness, even in the most familiar lessons;
- are avid readers of educational research and practice journals and other resources;
- actively participate in team meetings with colleagues, professional development sessions, and other opportunities to learn new ideas and strategies they can implement in their practice;
- contribute to and learn from online communities for educators;
- recognize that coaching and mentoring relationships are mutually beneficial (whether they are the mentor or mentee, they embrace the opportunity to learn with and from their colleague);

- make the most of collegial interactions to share their own experiences and learn from others in the implementation of new curricular requirements and standards; and
- embrace the need to develop and maintain their "adaptive expertise" to continually improve their practice.

Through the use of these strategies, teachers truly develop wisdom by using feedback and shared professional expertise to improve.

GUIDING QUESTION ON LEARNING FROM EXPERIENCE

- What might we do differently next time so that we continuously improve our teaching practice?

Cognitive Asset 6: Maintaining Practical Optimism Throughout the Metacognitive, Collaborative Process

Developing and maintaining the cognitive asset of practical optimism, "an approach to life that focuses on taking practical positive action to increase the probability of successful outcomes" (Wilson & Conyers, 2011b, p. 148), is an overarching component of a metacognitive approach to teaching and leading. The next chapter will explore in more depth the impact of practical optimism in teacher leadership and purposeful collaboration; for now, it is important to note that developing an optimistic outlook is a crucial aspect of being metacognitive—and a difference maker in effecting positive change in our professional practice and in a school's learning environment. In short, it is not only possible—it is desirable—to enhance our positivity, and doing so can improve student learning outcomes and collegial interactions.

A positive orientation can be a powerful influence on teacher leaders' effectiveness as they work together. In particular, when educators agree that a positive approach to teaching and interacting with students can improve their practice, this shared belief may be self-fulfilling. As York-Barr, Sommerness, and Hur note:

> Teacher leaders who hold positive beliefs about the inner desire of people to learn, to feel competent, and to be socially connected are well situated to persist in making connections. Such persistence with grown-ups sometimes results in engagement and transformation, just as it does with children. (2008, p. 15)

A positive outlook can help veteran teachers maintain a passion for their profession and allow beginning teachers to sustain their enthusiasm and commitment to become the best educators they can be. Even though the demands and pressures of teaching may make this profession stressful over time, educators sharing a mindset of practical optimism can better manage those stresses and channel their energies in productive directions, especially when they receive positive reinforcers that are personally meaningful, rewarding, relevant, and enjoyable from colleagues and administrators (Louis, 2006).

GUIDING QUESTION ON PRACTICAL OPTIMISM

- As I interact with students, colleagues, administrators, and parents, how am I using and modeling practical optimism?

CONSTRUCTIVE CONCLUSIONS:
THE POWER OF WORKING SMARTER THROUGH METACOGNITION

In the endless complexities involved in teaching, purposeful collaboration, and leadership, developing a metacognitive mindset can help you continually improve your professional practice by:

1. Developing your clear intent in both your teaching and your collaborating and interacting with peers, administrators, and parents;
2. Keeping learning goals at the core of instructional planning and optimizing opportunities for collaborative unit and curricular planning;
3. Monitoring student progress, the effectiveness of your instructional techniques and strategies, and the outcomes of collaboration, mentoring, and coaching;
4. Engaging in productive evaluations of your professional practice and in seeking out input and feedback from colleagues;
5. Learning from experience in the classroom and from the collaborative work of teams of educators in your school and district; and
6. Developing practical optimism to elevate the positive learning environment of your school and collegial relationships among teachers and administrators.

Rather than finite and contained stages, these six strategies to increase metacognition in teaching and leadership are overlapping and interwoven. For example, Georgia middle school teacher Mary Leigh O'Connor notes that developing one's instructional repertoire to include strategies like these pays a dividend in enhancing positive outlook about students' ability to succeed academically: "I am now more optimistic because I believe that there will be something—a particular strategy, tip, or technique—that will enable students to unlock their own learning."

One path to working smarter is to aim for steady improvements, or "short-term wins," on which schools and districts can keep building, similar to the concept of incremental learning. Toward this end, becoming more metacognitive about your teaching, collaboration, and leadership opportunities takes a variety of forms in seeking evidence about what works in your classroom by reflecting on your practice and in supporting colleagues to adopt research-based strategies, measure their effectiveness in practice, and identify both ineffective and successful ideas. Strategies for teachers to encourage and support each other's positive outlooks for positive change in their classrooms and schools are shared in the next chapter.

CHAPTER 5

Encouraging a Supportive Culture for Learning and Teaching

Highly successful teacher leaders . . . exude optimism and a "can do" attitude that is contagious.

—Frank Crowther, Margaret Ferguson, & Leonne Hann, 2009

Teacher leaders who model an optimistic attitude and actively encourage and support their colleagues can have a powerful positive influence on the attitudes and, ultimately, the professional practice of their peers. Donna is among those fortunate educators who credit a particular senior colleague with having inspired and helped her develop foundational strengths at the start of her career in education as an elementary school teacher:

Frances Higgins offered much-needed and appreciated advice and support. She modeled useful teaching strategies, observed in my classroom, and gave constructive, encouraging feedback that made a world of difference in my teaching and outlook about education. By attending professional development events on her own time and making the most of school days designated for professional learning, Frances also epitomized teaching as a lifelong learning process. I felt very special when she invited me to attend a national conference with her in a neighboring state, where we both learned new strategies to guide struggling readers to develop the skills they would need to thrive in our classrooms and throughout their years in school.

Frances Higgins's willingness to serve as a role model, mentor, and caring colleague exemplifies encouragement, the fourth component in our POWER model for teacher leadership. This form of leadership can bring out the best in all of us:

Just ask people who regularly achieve peak performance what the key to their success is. Like happy people, most often they will tell you about a person—a

parent, a coach, a teacher, a partner, a spouse, a manager early in their careers—who believed in them and drew out of them more than they knew
they had. That's the magical power in connection. (Hallowell, 2011, p. 81)

Hallowell touches on intertwined themes we will explore in this
chapter—the positive impact teacher leaders can achieve through encouraging and collaborating with colleagues and modeling an outlook
of practical optimism. The phrase "leading from the teachers' lounge"
refers to the sometimes-unintentional role educators collectively play
in influencing school culture. The impact of teachers' attitudes about
their profession, their school, their colleagues, and their students may
be positive or negative. Maintaining and modeling an optimistic outlook in the midst of the many challenges facing educators today is not
always easy, but the rewards can be far-reaching for both teachers and
their students.

Veteran and beginning teachers alike have much to contribute toward fostering an atmosphere of positive collegiality. Johnson (2012)
notes that "new teachers especially seem to crave and value advice from
colleagues, and they are more likely to see collaboration with other
teachers as an element that contributes to their success" (p. 56). At the
same time, the enthusiasm of teachers at the beginning of their careers
and their grounding in recent advances in research can inspire and inform the practice of their more experienced peers. Encouragement may
take many forms as teachers work together, offer support and empathy
for colleagues, and remain open to sharing with and learning from their
peers.

This chapter explores research supporting the premise that people
with a can-do approach are more likely to achieve the goals they set for
themselves than those with a pessimistic outlook. Equally as important
are findings that you are not born to be either an optimist or a pessimist.
Making a conscious effort to model practical optimism and support a
positive school culture can be transformational for you, your colleagues,
and your students, as embodied in the concept of *academic optimism*.
Adopting practical optimism as your modus operandi and taking advantage of opportunities to build rapport with colleagues and encourage
them to continually hone their professional practice in positive ways will
further enhance your emotional intelligence. You will improve relation-
ship-building and communication skills that support empathetic, productive interactions with colleagues, administrators, and parents. Two prime
responsibilities of teacher leaders are "driving the collective emotions in
a positive direction and clearing the smog created by toxic emotions"
(Goleman, Boyatzis, & McKee, 2002, p. 5).

THE POWER OF PRACTICAL OPTIMISM

Positive emotion is essential to effective teaching and successful learning. In the past, learning was believed to stem solely from the exercise of intellect and cognitive processes, with no role for emotions. Recent research, however, shows that emotional and social functions play crucial roles in education. In an article titled "We Feel, Therefore We Learn," Immordino-Yang and Damasio note that "the neurobiological evidence suggests that the aspects of cognition that we recruit most heavily in schools, namely learning, attention, memory, decisionmaking, and social functioning, are both profoundly affected by and subsumed within the processes of emotion" (2007, p. 3). The interconnections of emotions and education are at work for both teachers and students (Immordino-Yang, 2015).

We now know an optimistic outlook with an expectation that you can accomplish a learning goal increases the likelihood that you will attain it—and you are more likely to be optimistic if you have people who care about and support you by encouraging you to put in the hard work and persistent effort that may be required along the way.

We refer to *practical optimism,* which goes beyond simply putting on a happy face to entail taking positive action to increase the probability of successful outcomes (Wilson & Conyers, 2011b). A sunny, enthusiastic disposition is not mandatory for adopting this approach (although some practical optimists certainly exhibit these traits). Instead, practical optimism is characterized by a belief—in yourself and others—that success is possible, which in turn fuels determination to accomplish what you have set out to do.

The field of positive psychology grew out of research that demonstrates the power of an optimistic outlook. Extensive study and teaching by Martin Seligman (2002, 2011b), one of the foremost proponents of positive psychology, suggests that we can learn to become more optimistic, and his research offers an incentive for doing so: Optimists may live longer on average than their pessimistic peers, and they tend to be healthier and more successful and experience greater enjoyment of life.

A shared positive outlook can also transform the workplace. As a Wall Street Journal article (Pryce-Jones, 2012) reports, "Happier workers help their colleagues 33% more than their least happy colleagues; raise issues that affect performance 46% more; achieve their goals 31% more; and are 36% more motivated." Other studies have found that employees with an optimistic outlook were 12% more productive than their pessimistic counterparts (Oswald, Proto, & Sgroi, 2014) and that people who exude happiness are more likely to get second interviews (Burger & Caldwell, 2000).

Many authors have cited the power of positivity in our personal and professional lives. For example, in *The Winner's Brain*, Brown and Fenske suggest that one attribute of successful people is "opportunity radar," or the ability to find "solutions when none seem to exist," to see possibilities for gains even in setbacks, and to always be on the lookout for new ways to come at stubborn problems (2010, p. 31). Their exploration of the attributes of people who seem to be wired for success reflects the central message of positive psychology:

> If you sit around and mope because something doesn't go your way, this mindset may have an ongoing effect on your brain's activity. If you continue to brood day after day, these patterns can lead to ingrained changes in the neural structures themselves. (Indeed long-term stress and depression can cause areas of the brain to shrink, particularly the hippocampus.) Just as repeatedly engaging in negative thoughts and action can lead to undesirable brain alterations, actively engaging in more positive thoughts and actions can lead to beneficial ones. Thus, you can take control of your brain and overhaul your life. . . . [The brains of successful people] take control over plasticity by intentionally making the changes they want, and they deliberately take the steps to think and act in ways that fine-tune their brains and help to achieve their goals. (p. 160)

Brown and Fenske also put forward the concept of "optimal emotional balance." Achieving peak emotional balance entails three aims: "recognizing emotions in yourself and others; predicting what emotional response you'll have in a given circumstance; and the art of adjusting your emotions accordingly to get what you want" (p. 114). As with practical optimism, you can learn to achieve emotional balance. Purposefully regulating your emotions can be an advantage in both your work and personal lives, particularly when confronted with situations beyond your control.

People with an optimistic outlook are more likely to be undaunted by setbacks and challenges and to keep trying until they succeed. Their perseverance is fueled by their beliefs that they will prevail over adversity, learn from their failures, and overcome plateaus in performance and progress. On the other hand, pessimists are more likely to give up, drop out, and doubt their abilities. They tend to internalize setbacks and view challenges as permanent and insurmountable. Where pessimists see obstacles as a reason to quit, optimists see one more task to complete, one more puzzle to solve on the road to success.

Applying these findings about practical optimism to teacher leadership, your outlook, attitudes about your individual and collective impact on student outcomes, and the joy you find in your profession help to set the tone in your school. Crowther and colleagues (2009) relate how conscious efforts by teachers at a rural high school to develop a collective "'we can do anything' attitude . . . had a demonstrable impact on student's self-esteem and achievements. Even seemingly insignificant achievements were held up as evidence that all students can achieve beyond normal expectations when they are encouraged and recognized" (p. 18). In the wake of establishing this new positive learning environment, the school "has achieved marked recognition for its academic, cultural, and sporting successes" (p. 5). A teacher there described the turnaround in behavior that resulted in classroom 9D when he asked students to share their ideas of what makes a good lesson. By applying the "9D Statement of Good Teaching and Learning" the students developed, "lessons were so much more productive—and fun—for all, a very supportive class culture developed and academic results improved" (p. 7).

In synthesizing more than 800 meta-analyses, educational researcher John Hattie (2009) found ample evidence for the role of an optimistic teaching approach in supporting learning. Summarizing some of that research, he writes that creating a positive learning environment:

> requires teachers to enter the classroom with certain conceptions about progress, relationships, and students. It requires them to believe that their role is that of a change agent—that all students *can* learn and progress, that achievement for all is changeable and not fixed, and that demonstrating to all students that they care about their learning is both powerful and effective. (p. 128)

Nurturing Your Inner Optimist

In short, developing practical optimism and modeling this approach for colleagues, administrators, parents, and others can have a positive impact on both school climate and student learning. To take full advantage of these findings, we may need to examine our own assumptions about the nature of optimism vs. pessimism. There is a common belief that people are either naturally optimistic or prone to pessimism, and that this is just the way things are. It turns out that this belief is *half* true: Research indicates that people's inherited "set point" or baseline accounts for about 50% of their emotional outlook, and another 10% stems from life circumstances, including socioeconomic, health, and relationship status. The remaining 40% is within people's ability to control, which Lyubomirsky (2007) refers to as "room to maneuver, for opportunities to increase or decrease our happiness levels through what we *do* in our daily lives and how we *think*" (p. 22).

It is possible to take conscious, proactive steps to foster more positive emotions, meaningful engagement in professional and personal pursuits, and positive relationships with family, friends, and colleagues. Nurturing your well-being involves committing your strengths and virtues, such as kindness, social intelligence, humor, courage, and integrity, "to meet the highest challenges that come your way. Deploying your highest strengths leads to more positive emotion, to more meaning, to more accomplishment, and to better relationships" (Seligman, 2011b, p. 24). We see good news for teachers in these findings: What better cause is there to commit your strengths and talents to than embracing purposeful collaboration and teacher leadership roles with the ultimate aim of improving student learning?

A variety of strategies may be useful in enhancing your practical optimism and sharing this approach with colleagues. Here are just a few:

Sharpen your focus on a positive outlook. Research indicates that wandering minds tend to gravitate toward negative thoughts and emotions (Killingsworth & Gilbert, 2010). By checking in randomly with more than 5,000 study participants around the world via a mobile phone app, Killingsworth and Gilbert found that, in a majority of those instances, people's minds were not on the task at hand and that "people were less happy when their minds were wandering than when they were not" (2010, p. 932). By committing conscious effort to focusing on the positive and productive, teachers can develop, maintain, and model greater optimism, which will in turn enhance their professional practice and interactions with colleagues and administrators. As we will discuss later in this chapter, maintaining an optimistic learning environment supports gains in students' academic performance and a more positive and productive work setting.

Hand in hand with a deliberate focus on a positive outlook is learning to let go of the negative. You may have seen this dynamic at work in some schools where you have taught: There is no shortage of issues to worry and fret about in teaching, and when negative attitudes and discussions dominate collegial interactions, the result can be a downward spiral. We are not suggesting practical optimism is a cure-all for the many challenges in education, but there is no doubt that a positive attitude provides a stronger foundation for confronting those challenges than a negative outlook. When something goes wrong, optimists aim to fix what is within their control and recognize what is not, to depersonalize setbacks, and to maintain a sense of perspective rather than blow problems out of proportion (Seligman, 2011b). From this more positive perspective, optimists are better able to step back from problems, consider possible solutions, and learn from their experiences.

Feel good by doing good. A wealth of research supports the positive boomerang impact of helping others: Committing small acts of kindness has been shown to enhance positive emotions and produce a long-term boost in well-being (e.g., Buchanan & Bardi, 2010; Dixon, 2011; Lyubomirsky, 2007). Deliberate and conscious altruism involving colleagues, students, family, friends, or strangers produces a variety of psychological benefits (Achor, 2010). Even small gestures, such as sharing specific praise for a colleague's teaching practice at a staff gathering or bringing healthy snacks to share at a team meeting, can decrease stress and make you feel good about yourself and those around you. A school atmosphere characterized by kindness in the classroom, between colleagues, and among administrators, teachers, and other school staff is high on empathy and supportive interactions and low on stress and anxiety.

Frequently say two simple words. "Thank you." Educational research on gratitude indicates that when students are encouraged to recognize and write about people who have made a positive difference in their lives, they are more optimistic and exhibit more pro-social behavior among peers (Froh & Bono, 2012). Among adults, active appreciation for what they have and what matters to them most supports a more positive attitude in their personal and professional lives. Davidson (2012a) suggests keeping track of how often you feel gratitude and expressing it sincerely and personally by looking the person in the eye. You might even want to keep a daily journal that notes how many times during each day you felt gratitude and how you felt in expressing it—to colleagues, support personnel, administrators, students, and school volunteers, as just a few examples.

Cultivate positive relationships with colleagues and celebrate their successes. As we have noted previously, many teachers count interactions with their peers as important sources of support and ideas to improve their practice. Beyond boosts in productivity, positive collegial relationships offer less tangible benefits—the feelings that "we're all in this together" and that together we can do much more than we can individually. Work friendships are worth investing time and effort to maintain. As Lyubomirsky (2007) advises,

> If you begin today to improve and cultivate your relationships, you will reap the gift of positive emotions. In turn, the enhanced feelings of happiness will help you attract more and higher-quality relationships, which will make you even happier, and so on, in a continuous positive feedback loop. (pp. 138–139)

An effective way to build solid work relationships is to recognize and celebrate your coworkers' successes. Sharing in the joy when your colleagues make gains in their professional practice elevates your school environment and helps shine the spotlight on effective teaching.

Consciously strive to enhance your resilience. Improving your professional practice and skills as a teacher leader does not always entail continuous forward progress. In any complex endeavor—and teaching is certainly that—there will be setbacks and difficulties. It is possible to enhance your resilience, recover more quickly from setbacks, and maintain your optimistic outlook in the face of adversity. In his research, Davidson (2012b) identified connections between the prefrontal cortex, which is associated with higher-order thinking, and the amygdala in the limbic system, which is known as the emotional center of the brain. These connections are activated by emotional responses of distress and anxiety. In his experiments, Davidson found that through mindfulness training, or focusing our thoughts on calming down in an adverse situation, we can train our brains to recover from distress more quickly "by weakening the chain of associations that keep us obsessing about and even wallowing in a setback."

Recognize your own special talents. One of the biggest benefits of purposeful collaboration and teacher leadership is that it brings the collective talents and expertise of an entire team to bear on the challenges of our profession. What personal and professional strengths do you bring to the table? Parlaying your strengths to maximum impact can boost your professional practice and provide additional support to your colleagues through mentoring, coaching, and collaboration. Recognizing and playing to your strengths can also make your work life more enjoyable and help you maintain a positive outlook. In the graduate studies program we codeveloped, many teachers have enjoyed learning about their signature strengths. Some teachers have even reported feeling transformed and rejuvenated by identifying their strengths and talents, and they say they have translated this exercise successfully for use with their students.

Move your body to boost your mood. Regular physical activity can help to alleviate depression, reduce stress, and diminish feelings of anxiety. This positive impact is nearly instantaneous: The mood-enhancing effects of exercise are typically felt during or within minutes after completing a workout (Weir, 2011). Including time for exercise in your daily routine will help maintain your optimistic outlook, relieve work-related stress, and help you sleep better.

Becoming more optimistic entails deliberate effort. And as with maintaining other competencies, sustaining a positive outlook may require a "practical maintenance routine" of being mindful of the good things in life, in you, in your work, and in students, colleagues, and administrators. Taken together, these strategies for enhancing your practical optimism can also help improve your emotional intelligence (EQ). This crucial form of intellectual development, which brings together thinking and feeling, "is the foundation for a host of critical skills—it impacts most everything you say and do each day. . . . It's the single biggest predictor of performance in the workplace and the strongest driver of leadership and personal excellence" (Bradberry & Greaves, 2009, pp. 20–21).

FOSTERING ACADEMIC OPTIMISM TO SUPPORT STUDENT ACHIEVEMENT

Reviewing several decades of research to identify the properties of schools and teachers related to student achievement, Hoy, Tarter, and Woolfolk Hoy (2006) suggest that only three factors are consistently connected with achievement (controlling for the effects of socioeconomic status): (1) the efficacy of faculty and individual teachers, (2) teachers' trust that students and their parents will respond in positive ways to educational endeavors, and (3) the academic emphasis of the school, where teachers put forth high, achievable goals and believe in all students' ability to succeed and where both educators and students respect high academic achievement. A unifying "construct" that supports all three of these factors is *academic optimism,* which brings together the cognitive aspect of self-efficacy (teachers' beliefs in their own ability to teach all students), the affective aspect of trust, and the behavioral elements of keeping the focus on academics. "Academic optimism is especially attractive because it emphasizes the potential of schools to overcome the power of socioeconomic factors that impair student achievement [and] attempts to explain and nurture what is best in schools to facilitate student learning" (Hoy et al., 2006, p. 443).

Academic optimism encompasses "teachers' beliefs about themselves, their students, and their instruction" and relates directly to "teachers' optimism about teaching and learning in their own school" (Woolfolk Hoy, 2012, p. 93). Several studies have linked academic optimism at the school level to student achievement in core subjects and at all grade levels, and research has begun to find evidence for the same connections at the individual teacher level. The main links that connect academic optimism to teacher efficacy, trust in students and parents, and academic emphasis are motivation and cooperation:

We theorize that being more academically optimistic allows teachers to set goals for themselves and their students that are specific and challenging, the kind of goals that support achievement. In addition, academically optimistic teachers accept responsibility for learning, are motivated to exert strong effort, persist in difficult tasks, and are resilient in the face of problems and failures. Finally, academic optimism encourages cooperation among students, teachers, and parents in matters of student learning, which enhances teacher and student motivation. (Woolfolk Hoy, 2012, p. 95)

As with more general forms of positive thinking, these educational researchers make the point that academic optimism can be learned. Toward that end, Woolfolk Hoy recommends that teacher education programs should underscore that educators can and should "self-regulate their efficacy" and "focus on strengths—of the teacher and of the students" (2012, p. 96). On your own, you can seek out research on content and pedagogical knowledge to enhance academic emphasis and study models of successful parent involvement programs. In addition, by reinforcing for your colleagues the potential gains that can be made by bringing together these components of effective schools, you can help contribute to academic optimism among teachers and students—and set the stage for advances in students' academic performance.

This conceptualization of academic optimism, with its foundation in effective teaching practice, trusting relationships with students and their parents, and a focus on learning, is consistent with research from the Wallace Foundation on school leadership. This research identifies essential components for educators and administrators working together to support student learning, including: (1) a vision for academic success for all students fueled by high expectations; (2) a school climate that emphasizes safety, cooperation, and fruitful interactions among principals, teachers, parents, and the wider community; (3) leadership opportunities for teachers with the aim of improving instruction (Mendels, 2012).

EMPATHY AS A KEY LEADERSHIP SKILL

Optimism is a hallmark of teacher leaders, who enhance their school's culture by encouraging and supporting their colleagues in positive ways. In a school climate that reflects feelings of security, trust, pride, unity, cooperation, and shared decisionmaking, teachers are more likely to be motivated to improve their professional skills (Watt & Richardson, 2013). Developing an empathetic approach to build rapport with colleagues is an effective way to help foster this positive, motivating environment and to become an influential advocate for improving one's practice (Katzenmeyer & Moller, 2009).

Goleman (2011, p. 61) suggests that it is possible to develop the "core skill" of empathy, which takes three forms: cognitive empathy ("I know how you see things; I can take your perspective"), emotional empathy (which he describes as "the basis for rapport and chemistry"), and empathic concern ("I sense you need some help and I spontaneously am ready to give it"). From these descriptions, it is easy to see how conveying an empathetic approach might enhance your influence with colleagues, administrators, and parents as you undertake leadership and collaboration roles. When you are able to develop sincere, positive connections with others, they are more likely to accept your encouragement and support and to listen to your ideas.

As colleagues develop rapport through empathetic interactions, they experience both cognitive and physiological responses. Think back to an interaction you've had with others in which you felt in total harmony. You might have been working on a home or work project together, playing a game, enjoying a concert, or just involved in deep, pleasant conversation. Goleman (2011, p. 57) notes that "these moments of interpersonal chemistry, or simpatico, are when things happen at their best." This "physiology of rapport" entails three components: paying full attention to one another, becoming physically in synch to the point of adopting the same gestures and facial expressions, and sharing positive feelings. Rapport does not happen automatically. Taking the time to convey empathy and getting to know the colleagues you are mentoring or working with in teams can help to make those work relationships more constructive and beneficial and further the positive climate in your school. Just as developing positive relationships with students supports learning, fostering an atmosphere of caring collegiality with your fellow teachers and administrators increases the likelihood that you will be able to take on the challenges of your profession together.

The impact of developing rapport with teaching colleagues is illustrated in a story shared by a teacher leader in Lieberman and Friedrich's *How Teachers Become Leaders* (2010). This teacher had served in a variety of leadership roles, including working as a demonstration teacher conducting seminars, workshops, and sample lessons and developing instructional resources for classroom teachers at schools throughout her district. But her perspective is that she had more influence on teachers' professional practice when she worked as a reading and writing coach in a single school, where she had the opportunity to get to know and develop relationships with teachers as they planned lessons together and the teachers became comfortable asking her for support, observation, and feedback. The most effective collaborative environments are those where teachers are encouraged and provided with opportunities to build rapport with their colleagues, she suggests:

> I work side-by-side with my peers. I make the work I do transparent during grade level and team meetings. Teachers observe, read student work on the walls, and ask for lesson plans, templates, or prompts that I use with my students. They come to me to ask for a book, discuss a genre, or ask how to help students revise their work; and this is my greatest compliment. I give it away, everything—my process, ideas, and suggestions—and it is reciprocated. I reveal my inadequacies and concerns, and they all know that I am with the team. As classroom teachers, we can talk about the joys and the struggles in teaching in a way where judgment is reserved and it is safe to be real. We have a learning community and we each value it. (p. 82)

A pervasive optimistic outlook among teachers supports a shared belief that all students can succeed. Over time, this positive outlook can become a self-fulfilling prophecy. By recognizing and encouraging improvements in learning and teaching rather than emphasizing shortcomings and setbacks, teacher leaders "enhance confidence, induce high expectations, and extend horizons for their students" (Crowther et al., 2009, p. 19).

CONSTRUCTIVE CONCLUSIONS: THE POWER OF ENCOURAGEMENT

"Perseverance, Respect, Positive Attitude" were the school values identified by teachers at Adams Secondary College (of grades 7–12 students) in Australia involved in an educational revitalization project (Crowther et al., 2009). To emphasize the role of teachers as "professional leaders," this project focused on the importance of teachers, both individually and collectively, in improving student outcomes; of professional learning and sharing success stories; and of collective responsibility for developing and implementing a new strategic direction for the school. The result of these collaborative efforts, which consistently integrated the identified core values of perseverance, respect, and positive attitude, was "enhanced confidence, clarified focus, and heightened expectations" for both teachers and their students in the form of improved morale, more positive learning environments, and higher motivation for learning among students (p. 25).

This example reflects the premise of this chapter: Teacher leaders encourage the adoption of and model practical optimism and high expectations—for themselves, their students, and their colleagues. This approach is consistent with Teacher Leadership Model Standard VI from the Teacher Leadership Exploratory Consortium, which calls for "improving outreach and positive collaboration with stakeholders in the learning community—families, community members and leaders, and others—in order to improve student learning and guide necessary change."

Modeling a positive outlook when collaborating with and mentoring colleagues and interacting with administrators and parents can counter negative, self-defeating attitudes. In addition, shared leadership and opportunities for positive collaboration alleviate feelings of isolation and burnout among teachers and help to elevate school climate. Here are some strategies for powering up with positivity in your school:

Shine the spotlight on classroom success stories. Encouraging educators to share effective teaching strategies (1) draws on research that teachers are comfortable learning from peers (and some may even prefer it), (2) emphasizes one of many forms of lifelong professional learning, (3) recognizes the contributions of all teachers to your professional learning community, and (4) provides an opportunity to celebrate these successes. To this final point, Kouzes and Posner (2012) note, "Celebrations and rituals, when they are authentic and from the heart, build a strong sense of collective identity and community spirit that can carry a group through extraordinarily tough times" (p. 24). A key leadership role is advocating for outlets for teachers to share their professional expertise; some possible outlets include dedicating the majority of staff meetings to presentations and discussions about effective teaching strategies, hosting district "science fairs" in which teachers share the results of their action research, and collaboratively developing "best-practices books" in which every teacher contributes one strategy, practice, or story (Reeves, 2008). These avenues for disseminating effective strategies support teachers in sharing and rediscovering the joy of teaching. "Strong teachers depend on other strong teachers for a constant sharing of ideas and resources" (Farr, 2010, p. 179).

Recognize and celebrate your colleagues' unique strengths and contributions. As we have noted throughout this text, teacher leadership takes many forms, requires different talents, and can be tailored to suit a variety of preferred methods of collaboration. Some teachers may look forward to making presentations to the school board, while others step forward to organize volunteer opportunities for parents and community members and still others prefer one-to-one mentoring with their peers. All of these contributions are valuable and deserving of recognition. As Farr (2010) notes, "Not all teachers are masters of all methods and resources, but most teachers have an area of strength to learn from" (p. 180).

Contribute to an environment in which teachers are confident and secure enough to offer feedback to colleagues and welcome suggestions from their fellow teachers. Peer reviews, observations in model classrooms, and visits to other schools provide potent professional learning opportunities. A "simple litmus test of highly effective teachers is that they, unlike less effective teachers, seek out critical friends who will offer fresh, objective, and constructive feedback on their teaching" (Farr, 2010, p. 180). By establishing rapport through empathetic interactions with colleagues, you can help foster a trusting, caring environment where teachers feel comfortable and confident in sharing and accepting guidance.

Spread the word about the power of practical optimism to support learning—to colleagues, principals, and parents. Teacher leaders can help set and maintain a productive and positive climate: Happy leaders have an impact on everyone with whom they interact because they help motivate others to set high goals and help encourage them along the way as they begin to reach their goals.

CHAPTER 6

Results of Effective Teacher Leadership

> High-performing states and nations are focused on building coherent *systems* of teaching and learning, focused on meaningful goals and supported with universally available, strategic resources.
>
> —Linda Darling-Hammond, 2011

The renowned business consultant and systems thinker W. Edwards Deming (1994) insisted that organizations must take a systems approach to improving the quality of their work; he estimated that 94% of problems are caused by the system and 6% by special causes. Throughout this text we have cited evidence of the gains that result when teachers and administrators work together to improve instructional practice at the school and district level rather than just in individual classrooms. A systematic approach to purposeful collaboration can create tremendous synergy to facilitate learning gains for virtually all students. Fullan cites research that supports the effectiveness of "coherent, consistent reform . . . implementing a small number of core priorities especially well" (2010, p. 55), with involvement from 90% or more teachers in a school or district. Tucker also underscores the need for a systems approach and, in his final comment below, suggests the need for clearer assumption of responsibility for system design, perhaps a vacuum that broader and stronger teacher leadership within a system might fill:

> The reality is that the outcomes we care about in education are the result of myriad variables, all interacting in ways we cannot possibly visualize or simulate in our computers, to produce the outcomes we see. Each program we evaluate with our sophisticated research techniques can actually be considered in real schools and school systems as one among many variables affecting the outcomes we care about. If no one thinks of themselves as responsible for the design of the overall system, then we should not be surprised that any single initiative or program, no matter how well conceived and executed, has a relatively small effect on student achievement. . . . The one thing that

could have a very large effect—the design of the system itself—is no one's responsibility. (2011, p. 205)

In this chapter we present the final component of the POWER framework—how purposeful collaboration and teacher leadership have contributed to positive results in successful school systems across the country and around the world. We also explore how educators and administrators can implement some of the collaborative and leadership strategies employed in those systems in their own schools and districts to continuously improve instruction.

APPLYING SOCIAL PHYSICS FOR POSITIVE CHANGE: BECOME A CHARISMATIC CONNECTOR

Chapter 3 introduced findings about collective intelligence, the enhanced creativity and problem solving that results from small groups of people working together effectively to generate ideas, reach agreement about possible solutions, and monitor results with an eye toward continual improvements. Research by social scientists in diverse work settings, from a call center to the sales support team of a computer company, concluded that work productivity and creative output are directly related to the amount of interactions colleagues have and their level of engagement, or idea flow among members in a work group (Pentland, 2014).

We believe these findings are directly applicable to school settings: In an environment with classroom after classroom of students, each with their unique own brain, a near-infinite assortment of novel teaching and learning challenges arises regularly. By advocating for and taking full advantage of adequate planning and discussion time with colleagues, teachers can productively share problems and ideas and come up with creative solutions. These regular interactions permit teachers "to alternate between exploration for idea discovery and engagement with others for behavior change" (Pentland, 2014, p. 97), which is at the core of social learning, creative problem solving, implementation, and long-term positive change. "The number of opportunities for social learning, usually through informal face-to-face interactions among peer employees, is often the largest single factor in company productivity" (p. 103). Thus, the persistent older model of American education—teachers isolated in their classrooms, rarely crossing paths with their colleagues to exchange ideas—is antithetical to putting social physics to work in support of effective teaching.

Pentland identifies the most effective style of leadership in fostering idea flow as people willing to develop their skills as "charismatic connectors":

> They are genuinely interested in everyone and everything. I think their real interest is in idea flow, although probably few would describe their interest that way. They tend to drive conversations, asking about what is happening in people's lives, how their projects are doing, how they are addressing problems, etc. The consequence is that they develop a good sense of everything that is going on and become a source of social intelligence. (2014, pp. 117–118)

That profile of charismatic connectors is quite similar to descriptions of effective administrators and teacher leaders. And like these educators, Pentland suggests, charismatic connectors employ skills and outlooks they have worked to develop, rather than rely on some innate predilection: being a good listener, demonstrating an interest and openness to other people's ideas and points of view, exhibiting empathy, and modeling practical optimism.

LESSON STUDY IN JAPAN:
OPTIMIZE GROUP PLANNING AND RESEARCH

Japan's students are perennially at the top of the Programme for International Student Assessment (PISA) for science and math and also do consistently well in reading (Tucker & Ruzzi, 2011). (PISA is an assessment of the language literacy, math, and science performance of 15-year-old students administered by the Organisation for Economic Co-operation and Development in 70 countries, including the United States.) One practice that distinguishes Japanese school systems and that has become a model for purposeful collaboration is known as Japanese Lesson Study.

Lesson study is a professional development process in which a small group of teachers formulate a research question related to a "study lesson" with the aim of improving their instructional practice and students' learning outcomes. The teachers work together to develop a detailed lesson plan and then observe as one of their team members teaches it in a classroom. The group may then revise the lesson and observe again as another teacher implements it.

This form of purposeful collaboration has drawn a great deal of interest for a variety of reasons. The research focus is selected and implemented by teachers themselves, rather than being imposed on them by outside entities, and is immediately relevant to their everyday practice. In other words, "it offers teachers the opportunity to develop professional communities of inquiry, with ownership of the improvement effort, a commitment to inquiry, shared goals, and a sense of responsibility to colleagues and their students" (Doig & Groves, 2011, p. 90). The process is relatively informal and adaptable and can bring together not only job-alike groups but also teachers from different grade levels and areas of practice to enhance the variety of perspectives and ideas available to address the problem and identify solutions. In short, lesson study exemplifies social physics in action.

Lesson study is among several aspects of the structure of the teaching profession that set the Japanese educational system apart from many American schools:

> Attention to the steady improvement of practice by the teachers themselves may be a powerful engine for improvement of student performance. Japan as a nation is a laboratory for the idea of continuous improvement of practice. The incarnation of that idea in Japanese schools is lesson study. This practice undoubtedly contributes in important ways to the high quality of instruction in Japanese schools. There is no reason that it could not be used all over the world. (Tucker & Ruzzi, 2011, p. 104)

Setting aside time in the school schedule for teachers' purposeful collaboration is crucial for lesson study and other educational approaches presented in this chapter to be effective pathways to improved instruction and student learning. Teachers in countries that value teacher collaboration and lesson study dedicate teacher time to permit these interactions, whereas U.S. teachers spend more time with students and have less time available to collaborate. Still, teachers and administrators in some districts in the U.S. have worked together to successfully incorporate more time for collaborative planning and professional learning into the school calendar (Killion, 2013). These collaborations are invested in improving lessons and in producing evidence of students' academic gains, and offer positive examples of the benefits of expanded shared planning and professional co-development.

Teacher leaders looking to implement the lesson study model in their schools might also benefit from developing their collaborative research skills. The Japanese teacher training system emphasizes "the kind of research skills needed to make sophisticated judgments about the effectiveness of their local development work," while in contrast, in U.S. schools, Tucker asserts, "teachers are generally the object of research rather than the participants themselves" (2011, p. 189). In fact, as we have noted, teacher leaders in the United States conduct action research to evaluate and improve their teaching and are adept Internet researchers in quest of best practices. Tucker adds that in successful school systems in other nations, "teachers are viewed as highly competent professionals who are expected to take the lead in defining what good practice is, advancing practice, and keeping up-to-date on the latest advances." This is the role that some teacher leaders play in their local schools and districts in the United States, with the commensurate local respect that accrues to such professionalism. However, at a national level, U.S. teachers are often seen as a workforce to be "managed," rather than as professionals to be respected, developed, and supported as in other countries, which makes the professional performance of teacher leaders and the few educational systems that support them the more to be admired.

BUILDING COLLECTIVE CAPACITY IN ONTARIO, CANADA: TAKE SOCIAL PHYSICS TO THE SYSTEMS LEVEL

Thus far we have discussed strategies to put social physics, practical applications to optimize collegial interactions, to work at the individual and small group levels in support of systemic change. The example of the York Region District School Board in southeastern Ontario demonstrates the power of building what Fullan (2010) refers to as *collective capacity* across a large school district. Student learning gains were especially striking in some of the York schools as a result of teachers and administrators working together to implement research-based educational reforms. In the Crosby Heights School for K–8 students in a low-income neighborhood, for example, scores on a provincial test more than doubled over three years: "reading scores went from 44% to 90%, reaching the ambitious provincial standard; writing went from 40% to 87%; and math went from 50% to 83% (as measured by the progress of the same cohort of students from Grade 3 to Grade 6)" (p. 45). In another York school that focused its efforts on improving academic performance among students considered at risk (students who are assessed to be at level 1 or 2 of a 4-point scale in terms of current achievement), the number of at-risk students dropped from 378 to 233 in a single year.

Fullan attributes these successes to a commitment on the part of teachers, administrators, and other school staff to build collective capacity through "a combination of strategies that excite people about moral purpose, focus capacity building, and above all develop a strong sense of partnership between the district and the schools, across schools, and between schools and the community" (p. 43). At the heart of this reform effort were the establishment of clear intent to improve instruction and the provision of professional development that was immediately relevant to achieving those goals.

Echoing the social physics research on collective intelligence, Fullan notes that "collective capacity is more than the sum total of individual capacities" (p. 45). The framework for building these combined capabilities includes professional learning and opportunities to collaborate and share ideas at the district level and in regional school clusters organized as "learning networks" (LNs), facilitating shared research and reporting of student results. A key aspect of those learning networks also reflects social physics research: "If you observe an LN session, you will see that no one dominates. They are co-learners, with practice and results as the drivers" (p. 48).

The experience of the York schools in enhancing student learning through purposeful collaboration of teachers and administrators is not isolated. In studies involving 1,000 4th- and 5th-grade teachers in a sample of 130 New York City schools, Leana (2011) reports on the differences between schools that exhibited high and low social capital, or the relative opportunities for teachers to share ideas and work together to solve problems that arise in their classrooms (see Chapter 3):

> Teacher social capital was a significant predictor of student achievement gains above and beyond teacher experience or ability in the classroom. And the effects of teacher social capital on student performance were powerful. If a teacher's social capital was just one standard deviation higher than the average, her students' math scores increased by 5.7%

As one teacher in this study put it: "Teaching is not an isolated activity. If it's going to be done well, it has to be done collaboratively over time."

THE "FINNISH DREAM" OF QUALITY EDUCATION FOR ALL: ADVOCATE FOR POSITIVE PROGRESS ACROSS SYSTEMS

Leadership and collaboration by effective teachers have played a central role in making the Finns world leaders in educational reform. Students consistently perform at or near the top in PISA surveys, in terms of both quality and equity: A great majority of Finnish students perform well on these assessments, regardless of socioeconomic status (Sahlberg, 2011). Dropout rates are low in Finland, and enrollment in higher education is commonplace.

Pasi Sahlberg, a Finnish teacher, teacher educator, and educational researcher, has written extensively about the three decades of educational reform to which his country committed, and the central role that teachers and administrators played in significant advances in student achievement. He notes that educational leaders applied research and models from other countries, adapting those findings into an approach that is uniquely Finnish:

> The Finnish Way of change preserves the best of traditions and present good practices, and combines it with innovations found from others. Cultivating trust, enhancing autonomy, and tolerating diversity are just some of the examples of change ideas that are found in Finnish schools today. Many pedagogical ideas and educational innovations are initially imported from other countries, often from North America or the United Kingdom. Those include curriculum models from England, California, and Ontario; cooperative learning from the United States and Israel; portfolio assessment from the United States; teaching of science and mathematics from England, the United States, and Australia; and peer-assisted leadership from Canada, to mention a few. At the same time, the Finnish Dream of education is "made in Finland" and therefore also owned by Finns rather than rented. (2011, p. 7)

The lessons learned from Finnish schools support the need for purposeful collaboration and leadership by educators. "Teachers have time to work together during a school day and understand how their colleagues teach. This is an important condition for reflecting on teachers' own teaching and also building shared accountability between teachers" (Sahlberg, 2011, p. 91). As with teacher education programs in Japan, the Finnish teacher education system focuses on the development of practical research skills to equip teachers to take on the roles of curriculum development, student assessment, and school improvement.

In sum, teaching in Finland "is based on collaboration rather than isolation, autonomy rather than top-down authority, and professional responsibility rather than bureaucratic accountability" (Sahlberg, 2013). A team approach among educators is commonplace, with teachers working together to develop curriculum, discuss individual support for students with special needs, and suggest and assess classroom learning activities.

KENNEWICK, WASHINGTON: LEAD THE WAY WITH TEACHER-LED PROFESSIONAL DEVELOPMENT

Teacher-led professional development and classroom observations facilitated by technology were useful tools in efforts to systematically improve instruction and student achievement throughout the Kennewick

School District in Washington (Fielding, Kerr, & Rosier, 2007). Over a decade, the rate of students meeting or exceeding federal math and reading goals increased from 57% to 89.9%. Shared clear intent to improve instruction, purposeful collaboration among teachers and administrators, and teacher leadership in the form of literacy coaches and mentors supported these gains.

Recognizing that "the best method for learning about quality instruction would be to study our best teachers" (Fielding et al., 2007, p. 64), the district sponsored instructional conferences five times a year with four sessions at each conference for administrators and teacher leaders, including reading instructors representing each elementary school, and middle and high school literacy coaches. The instructional conferences featured videotaped lessons from Kennewick classrooms, with split-screen views of teachers and students, to facilitate analysis and group discussions of student behaviors, learning outcomes, and post-lesson interviews with students to assess "whether their experience of the lesson correspond with intended learning" (p. 64).

Administrators and educators reviewing the most successful elements of Kennewick's school improvement processes identified granting more autonomy "to the people on site who are most affected by [instructional decisions]" (Fielding et al., 2007, p. 128), developing teacher leaders, operating peer assistance and review programs, and investing time and effort into the instructional conferences. One teacher leader commented on the importance of providing educators "many different avenues by which they can take leadership roles":

> They feel valued. I think teachers need to be involved in the whole process. If they're not part of the process, they could very well defy the process. The best possible way is to involve all of the parties. So when teachers become leaders and are seen as leaders, there is greater buy-in. (pp. 128–129)

PURPOSEFUL COLLABORATION IN APPLYING THE SCIENCE OF LEARNING

Around the world and closer to home, research highlights great gains in student learning when teachers work together to develop their understanding of mind, brain, and education findings and apply them both in the classroom and in their collective professional development. Let's conclude with a few pertinent examples of proven steps in that success.

Build school reform efforts on a solid pedagogical foundation. Students in Shanghai, China's largest city, outperformed students from other countries in reading, math, and science in the 2009 PISA, with the lowest rate of students scoring at levels 1 and 2 across those core subjects. (Fewer than 20% of Shanghai students scored at low levels in all three subject areas, compared to more than 40% of American students.) In addition, more than half of Shanghai students achieved high scores (levels 5 and 6) in math (Tucker, 2011, pp. 9–10). Researchers studying Shanghai's successful school reforms suggest that teachers' commitment to study mind, brain, and education findings and to work together to apply those findings effectively in the classroom have these vital components:

> (1) a critical mass of scholars who concentrated on the sciences of learning; (2) a framework based on learning that shapes the curriculum; (3) professional discussions among educators in the form of debates, seminars, forums, conferences, and experiments, where theories of learning are interpreted and translated into grassroots practices; (4) effective methods of dissemination . . . ; and (5) perception management to convince parents and the media of the value of the changes. (Cheng, 2011, pp. 42–43)

Another aspect of educational reforms in Shanghai, which is also supported by research from learning sciences, is that "students' academic achievements are not separate from the other aspects of their personal development—affective, physical, cultural, spiritual, and so on" (Cheng, 2011, p. 43). This finding suggests the need for classroom teachers to collaborate with phys ed., art, and music teachers to plan lessons and learning activities that support development of the whole child.

These lessons learned in Shanghai schools are consistent with a survey of American teachers who studied the science of learning in earning their graduate degrees. Teachers reported that their graduate studies gave them "the tools necessary to support and encourage students, teachers and administrators to promote higher levels of thinking and learning using Mind, Brain, and Education strategies and philosophies" (Germuth, 2012, p. 15) and opened their eyes to "the critical importance of understanding how the brain learns most effectively and how teachers can harness that understanding in their classrooms" (p. 17).

Spread the word about the power of metacognition to support teaching and learning. Texas teacher Diane Dahl taught her students cognitive and metacognitive strategies to enhance reading comprehension, including visualizing, questioning, tapping into their schema of existing knowledge, and monitoring for understanding. As a result, her students' reading levels increased, on average, 5 months in just 2 1/2 months. Dahl shared information about those results and the metacognitive strategies she taught students in her blog "For the Love of Teaching" (fortheloveofteaching. net), which led to productive conversations sharing additional ideas and classroom strategies with teachers in other states and countries. This is a great example of the type of action research that can improve teaching and learning and inspire other teachers to follow suit. In addition, as discussed in Chapter 4, becoming more metacognitive can also help teachers enhance their professional practice and collaborative and leadership skills.

Set high expectations for teaching and learning. As we noted in Chapter 5, maintaining a positive school culture supports a shared mindset among administrators and teachers that they can make a difference in students' lives and that all students can learn. This outlook of practical optimism reinforces the need to set high expectations for students to make academic gains and the need to teach in ways that facilitate that achievement. Math teachers at an ethnically diverse California high school collaborated to develop a mixed ability curriculum in algebra and geometry with the shared expectation that all students would be able to master the challenging course content. After taking the courses, students scored higher than peers at other schools on the state standardized test, and 41% went on to take calculus as seniors. Reflecting the importance of a positive outlook, 84% of students agreed with the statement, "Anyone can be good at math if they try," compared to 54% of students in traditional classes at the comparison schools (Pellegrino & Hilton, 2012, p. 88).

Opportunities for ongoing support and positive interactions with colleagues are a necessary component of guiding teachers to overcome sometimes deeply held assumptions about their students' learning potential—and their own teaching abilities. Hargreaves and Fullan share the personal story of an Ontario elementary teacher who participated in biweekly reviews with colleagues to focus on students' learning outcomes and strategies for improvement. The 4th-grade teacher admits that she began attending these sessions only because "my principal sent me." After the first session, she recalls,

> I knew I should not have come. I looked at examples of Grade 4 student work from other teachers and I felt really badly. I had been teaching for years and knew my students could never produce such high quality writing. I did my best, though, to follow the process, feeling sick at heart for my kids. As the cycle progressed my classroom soared. Every one of my kids (who had been at Level 2) has produced writing at the high end of Level 3, some at Level 4. For 25 years of teaching I have set our goals too low. How many more of my students could have reached so much higher if only I had known I could take them there? (2012, pp. 55–56)

How many more teachers like this one continue to labor in isolation and near despair? Through purposeful collaboration, more teachers can access the support and shared professional development they need to transform their teaching and student learning.

Forge strong partnerships between administrators and teachers. Buy-in for teacher leadership and participation by administrators alongside teacher leaders and educators engaging in purposeful collaboration are crucial for the success of efforts to improve instruction and student outcomes. In one district in England, for example, teachers in eight disadvantaged schools received government grants for a school improvement project for 3 years, but funds for the project were ultimately pulled because the schools could not identify student achievement gains. Researchers identified lack of support by administrators as a key aspect of those stalled efforts (Owens, 2015). In contrast, other British studies have found that administrators (or "headteachers") sharing leadership responsibilities "can make a huge difference inside the classroom," especially when the shared leadership model "involved teachers, support staff, students, parents, and others in the community" (p. 147).

Specifically, teachers who took on leadership roles as part of shared leadership initiatives reported that school environments are most conducive to teacher leadership and collaboration when administrators recognize the gains that are possible through teacher leadership and when teachers are provided time and access for external support to carry out teacher-led development work. In short, this research concludes that "promoting and creating an environment conducive to the development of teacher leaders is crucial to improving schools, leadership, and learning" (Owens, 2015, p. 148).

Encourage "all-in" involvement and a shared commitment to systemic improvement. Returning to the concept introduced at the beginning of this chapter, teacher leadership and purposeful collaboration have the greatest impact on improving student achievement in schools and districts where *everyone* gets behind those efforts. This shared commitment was an essential element in the transformation of teaching and learning in the Norfolk Public Schools in Virginia: In 1998, only 11% of the city's elementary schools had more than half of their students reading at the proficient level; within 7 years, all of the schools had achieved that benchmark. By 2007, the district had made even more significant gains: All of its high schools improved in writing assessments, world history, and biology; all middle schools improved in math, and the great majority made gains in English literature test scores. In addition, "the equity gap has closed to zero in some schools," and "more than 20 percent more minority students took and passed advanced placement examinations compared with the previous year" (Reeves, 2008, p. 53).

Reeves suggests that the Norfolk story exemplifies the gains that result when an entire district commits "to a transparent, consistent focus on improved student achievement based on systematic, continuous changes in teaching and leadership practice" (2008, p. 52). Teachers were willing and ready to step up and take on leadership responsibilities, to learn from each other and from best practices in other schools, to serve as coaches, and to accept feedback on their professional practice. The district listened to and acted on their ideas, supported their leadership, encouraged innovation, and showcased successful teachers and teaching practices.

WHEN EDUCATORS LEAD THE WAY

The positive impacts on student learning reported by Norfolk Public Schools and other educational systems featured in this chapter highlight the gains that are possible when teachers and administrators engage in purposeful collaboration with a shared commitment to improving students' academic performance. As the spectrum of teacher leadership discussed throughout this book demonstrates, the roles educators may undertake toward this end are diverse and extend well beyond formal leadership appointments. American schools and the children they are entrusted with need collaborative teacher leaders, and teachers are inviting and accepting this challenge. In a forum held by the Association for Supervision and Curriculum Development (ASCD) on teacher leadership (ASCD Policy Points, 2014), "other leadership responsibilities" was the most common category teachers selected in a survey about the roles they hold outside the classroom, and "collaborative" was the most common term used in conversations about teacher leadership. These responses underscore two central points of this book: (1) leadership roles often defy simple categorization, and (2) student learning improves when teachers have ample opportunities to collaborate and support each other in becoming the best educators they can be. Teacher leaders are action researchers, mentors of colleagues just entering the profession, presenters of professional development events in their schools and districts, peer reviewers and coaches, parent educators, and tireless advocates for effective educational policies and practices.

Above all, teacher leaders are professional learners, adding to their tool kit of effective instructional strategies throughout their careers. In describing their "theory of change," Wagner and Kegen argue that "students' achievement will not improve unless and until we create schools and districts where all educators are learning how to significantly improve their skills as teachers and as instructional leaders" (2006, p. 23).

The true POWER of teacher leadership can be found in realizing the potential of our "plastic" brains to continually hone our professional practice, in taking advantage of opportunities for purposeful collaboration, in working smarter by developing a metacognitive approach to teaching and leading, in encouraging our colleagues to maintain a practically optimistic school culture, and in continually striving for positive results in student learning outcomes. Exciting new research holds great promise for teacher leaders today—and for their students and society at large.

References

Achor, S. (2010). *The happiness advantage: The seven principles of positive psychology that fuel success and performance at work.* New York, NY: Crown Business.

Aguilar, E. (2013). *The art of coaching: Effective strategies for school transformation.* San Francisco, CA: Jossey-Bass.

Alloway, T., & Alloway, R. (2013). *The new IQ: Use your working memory to think stronger, smarter, faster.* London, UK: HarperCollins.

ASCD Policy Points. (2014, November). The teacher leadership landscape. Available at ascd.org/ASCD/pdf/siteASCD/publications/policypoints/Teacher-Leadership-Nov-2014.pdf

Barth, R. S. (2006, March). Improving relationships within the schoolhouse. *Educational Leadership, 63*(6), 8–13.

Begley, S. (2012, January 19). The brain: How the brain rewires itself. *Time.* Available at content.time.com/time/magazine/article/0,9171,1580438,00.html

Berger, J. G. (2003). A summary of constructive-developmental theory of Robert Kegan. Available at wiki.canterbury.ac.nz/download/attachments/6358104/berger+on+kegan+narrative.doc?version=1.

Berliner, D. (2009). Research, policy, and practice: The great disconnect. In S. D. Lapan & S. D. Quartaroli (Eds.), *Research essentials: An introduction to designs and practices* (pp. 295–313). San Francisco, CA: Jossey-Bass.

Berninger, V. W., & Richards, T. L. (2002). *Brain literacy for educators and psychologists.* San Diego, CA: Academic Press/Elsevier Science.

Berry, B. (2014, October 21). Clearing the way for teacher leadership. *Education Week.* Available at edweek.org/ew/articles/2014/10/22/09berry.h34.html

Berry, B., Daughtrey, A., & Wieder, A. (2009, December). *Collaboration: Closing the effective teaching gap.* Carrboro, NC: Center for Teaching Quality. Available at teachingquality.org/content/collaboration-closing-effective-teaching-gap

Boone, S. C. (2015). Teacher leaders as school reformers. In N. Bond (Ed.), *The power of teacher leaders: Their roles, influence, and impact* (pp. 105–119). New York, NY: Routledge.

Bradberry, T., & Greaves, J. (2009). *Emotional intelligence 2.0*. San Diego, CA: TalentSmart.

Bransford, J., Brown, A., & Cocking, R. (Eds.). (2000). *How people learn: Brain, mind, experience, and school* (Expanded ed.). Washington, DC: National Academies Press.

Bransford, J., Darling-Hammond, L., & LePage, P. (2005). Introduction. In L. Darling-Hammond & J. Bransford (Eds.), *Preparing teachers for a changing world: What teachers should learn and be able to do* (pp. 1–39). San Francisco, CA: Wiley.

Brenneman, R. (2015, February 18). Seeking greater influence, teachers gain policy foothold in Education Department. *Education Week*. Available at http://www.edweek.org/tm/articles/2015/02/18/seeking-greater-influence-teachers-gain-policy-foothold.html

Brown, J., & Fenske, M. (2010). *The winner's brain: Eight strategies great minds use to achieve success*. Cambridge, MA: Da Capo Press.

Buchanan, K. E., & Bardi, A. (2010). Acts of kindness and acts of novelty affect life satisfaction. *Journal of Social Psychology, 150*(3), 235–237.

Burger, J. M., & Caldwell, D. F. (2000). Personality, social activities, job-search behavior, and interview success: Distinguishing between PANAS trait positive affect and NEO extraversion. *Motivation and Emotion, 24,* 51–62.

Chang, D. (2013, November 8). 9 reasons great teachers make great leaders. *Huffington Post Impact* [weblog]. Available at huffingtonpost.com/deborah-chang/9-reasons-great-teachers-_b_4236859.html

Cheng, K. (2011). Shanghai: How a big city in a developing country leaped to the head of the class. In M. S. Tucker (Ed.), *Surpassing Shanghai: An agenda for American education built on the world's leading systems* (pp. 21–50). Cambridge, MA: Harvard Education Press.

Christenbury, L. (2010, December/2011, January). The flexible teacher. *Educational Leadership, 68*(4), 46–50. Available at ascd.org/publications/educational-leadership/dec10/vol68/num04/The-Flexible-Teacher.aspx

Cohen, D. K., & Spillane, J. P. (1992). Policy and practice: The relations between governance and instruction. *Review of Research in Education, 18,* 3–49.

Cohen, S., & Janicki-Deverts, D. (2009, July). Can we improve our physical health by altering our social networks? *Perspectives on Psychological Science, 4*(4), 375–378.

Coleman, J. S. (1988). Social capital in the creation of human capital. *The American Journal of Sociology, 94,* S95–S120. Available at onemvweb.com/sources/sources/social_capital.pdf

Committee on the Study of Teacher Preparation Programs in the United States & the National Research Council. (2010). *Preparing teachers: Building evidence for sound policy*. Washington, DC: National Academies Press.

Conley, S., & Muncey, D. (2011). Teachers talk about teaming and leadership in their work. In E. Blair-Hilty (Ed.), *Teacher leadership: The "new" foundations of teacher education* (pp. 131–141). New York, NY: Peter Lang.

Conyers, M. A., & Wilson, D. L. (2015). *Positively smarter: Science and strategies for increasing happiness, achievement, and well-being.* West Sussex, UK: Wiley Blackwell.

Costa, A. L., Garmston, R. J., & Zimmerman, D. P. (2014). *Cognitive capital: Investing in teacher quality.* New York, NY: Teachers College Press.

Cozolino, L. (2014). *The neuroscience of human relationships: Attachment and the developing social brain* (2nd ed.). New York, NY: Norton.

Crowther, F., Ferguson, M., & Hann, L. (2009). *Developing teacher leaders* (2nd ed.). Thousand Oaks, CA: Corwin Press.

Dahl, D. (2011, March 31). Reading levels jump 5 months in just 2.5 months. Available at fortheloveofteaching.net/2011/03/reading-levels-jump-5-months-in-just-25.html

Danielson, C. (2007). The many faces of leadership. *Educational Leadership, 65*(1), 14–19.

Darling-Hammond, L. (2010). *The flat world and education: How America's commitment to equity will determine our future.* New York, NY: Teachers College Press.

Darling-Hammond, L. (2011). Foreword. In M. S. Tucker (Ed.), *Surpassing Shanghai: An agenda for American education built on the world's leading systems* (pp. ix–xii). Cambridge, MA: Harvard Education Press.

Darling-Hammond, L. (2013). *Getting teacher evaluation right: What really matters for effectiveness and improvement.* New York, NY: Teachers College Press.

Darling-Hammond, L., & Rothman, R. (2015). *Teaching in the flat world: Learning from high-performing systems.* New York, NY: Teachers College Press.

Davidson, R. J., with Begley, S. (2012a). *The emotional life of your brain.* New York, NY: Hudson Street Press.

Davidson, R. J. (2012b, February 21). Tired of feeling bad? The new science of feelings can help. *Newsweek.* Available at newsweek.com/tired-feeling-bad-new-science-feelings-can-help-65743

Deming, W. E. (1994). *The new economics for industry, government, and education* (2nd ed.). Cambridge, MA: MIT Press.

Derrington, M. L., & Angelle, P. S. (2013, Fall). Teacher leadership and collective efficacy: Connections and links. *International Journal of Teacher Leadership, 4*(1).

DeWitt, P. (2014, December 29). Teacher leadership is more complicated than you think. *Education Week.* Available at http://blogs.edweek.org/

edweek/finding_common_ground/2014/12/teacher_leadership_is_more_complicated_than_you_think.html

Dixon, A. (2011, September 6). Kindness makes you happy . . . and happiness makes you kind. Retrieved from *Greater Good: The Science of a Meaningful Life*, University of California, Berkeley, greatergood.berkeley.edu/article/item/kindness_makes_you_happy_and_happiness_makes_you_kind

Doig, B., & Groves, S. (2011). Japanese lesson study: Teacher professional development through communities of inquiry. *Mathematics Teacher Education and Development, 13*(1), 77–93.

Drago-Severson, E. (2008, Fall). Four practices serve as pillars for adult learning. *Journal of Staff Development, 29*(4), 60–63.

Drago-Severson, E. (2010). *Leading adult learning: Supporting adult development in our schools*. Thousand Oaks, CA: Corwin Press.

Drago-Severson, E. (2012). The need for principal renewal: The promise of sustaining principals through principal-to-principal reflective practice. *Teachers College Record*. Available at tcrecord.org/Content.asp?ContentId=16717

DuFour, R., & Fullan, M. (2013). *Cultures built to last: Systemic PLCs at work*. Bloomington, IN: Solution Tree Press.

Erickson, K. I., Oberlin, L., Swathi, G., Lecki, R. L., Weinstein, A. M., Hodzic, J. C., Wollam, M. E. (2014). Exercise as a way of capitalizing on neuroplasticity in late adulthood. *Topics in Geriatric Rehabilitation, 30*(1), 8–14.

Ericsson, K. A., Prietula, M. J., & Cokely, E. T. (2007, July–August). The making of an expert. *Harvard Business Review*. Available at 141.14.165.6/users/cokely/Ericsson_Preitula_&_Cokely_2007_HBR.pdf

Farr, S. (2010). Leadership not magic. *The Effective Educator, 68*(4), 28–33. Available at ascd.org/publications/educational-leadership/dec10/vol68/num04/Leadership,-Not-Magic.aspx

Feiman-Nemser, S. (2012). *Teachers as leaders*. Cambridge, MA: Harvard Education Press.

Felver, J. C., Doerner, E., Jones, J., Kaye, N. C., & Merrell, K. W. (2013). Mindfulness in school psychology: Applications for intervention and professional practice. *Psychology in the Schools, 50*(6), 531–547.

Fielding, L., Kerr, N., & Rosier, P. (2007). *Annual growth for all students: Catch-up growth for those who are behind*. Kennewick, WA: New Foundation Press.

Fleming, S. M. (2014, September/October). The power of reflection: Insight into our own thoughts, or metacognition, is key to higher achievement in all domains. *Scientific American*, 31–37.

Fotuhi, M. (2013). *Boost your brain: The new art and science behind enhanced brain performance*. New York, NY: HarperOne.

Froh, J. J., & Bono, G. (2012, November 19). How to foster gratitude in schools. *Greater Good: The Science of a Meaningful Life*. Available at greatergood.berkeley.edu/article/item/how_to_foster_gratitude_in_schools

Fullan, M. (2010). *All systems go: The change imperative for whole system reform.* Thousand Oaks, CA: Corwin Press.

Fullan, M. (2014). *The principal: Three keys for maximizing impact.* San Francisco, CA: Jossey-Bass.

Garmston, R. J. (2013). Developing smart groups. In A. L. Costa & P. W. O'Leary (Eds.), *The power of the social brain: Teaching, learning, and independent thinking* (pp. 75–83). New York, NY: Teachers College Press.

Germuth, A. A. (2012). *Empowering teacher leaders: The impact of graduate programs connecting mind, brain, and education research to teacher leadership.* Orlando, FL: BrainSMART.

Goddard, R. D., & Goddard, Y. L. (2001). A multilevel analysis of the relationship between teacher and collective efficacy in urban schools. *Teaching and Teacher Education, 17*(7), 807–818.

Goddard, R. D., Hoy, W. K., & Hoy, A. W. (2000). Collective teacher efficacy: Its meaning, measure, and impact on student achievement. *American Educational Research Journal 37*(2), 479–507.

Goddard, R. D., Hoy, W. K., & Woolfolk Hoy, A. (2004). Collective efficacy: Theoretical development, empirical evidence, and future directions. *Educational Researcher, 33,* 3–13.

Goleman, D. (2011). *The brain and emotional intelligence: New insights.* Northampton, MA: More Than Sound.

Goleman, D., Boyatzis, R., & McKee, A. (2002). *Primal leadership: Realizing the power of emotional intelligence.* Boston, MA: Harvard Business School Press.

Haberman, M. (1995). *STAR teachers of children in poverty.* West Lafayette, IN: Kappa Delta Pi.

Hallowell, E. M. (2011). *Shine: Using brain science to get the best from your people.* Boston, MA: Harvard Business Press.

Hamilton, J. (2008, October 2). Think you're multitasking? Think again. National Public Radio. Available at npr.org/templates/story/story.php?storyId=95256794

Hargreaves, A. (2015). Foreword. In N. Bond (Ed.), *The power of teacher leaders: Their roles, influence, and impact* (pp. x–xiii). New York, NY: Routledge.

Hargreaves, A., & Fullan, M. (2012). *Professional capital: Transforming teaching in every school.* New York, NY: Teachers College Press.

Harrison, C., & Killion, J. (2007). Ten roles for teacher leaders. *Educational Leadership, 65*(1), 74–77. Available at http://www.ascd.org/publications/educational-leadership/sept07/vol65/num01/Ten-Roles-for-Teacher-Leaders.aspx

Hartman, H. J. (2002). Teaching metacognitively. In H. J. Hartman (Ed.), *Metacognition in learning and instruction: Theory, research, and practice* (pp. 149–164). Dordrecht, Netherlands: Kluwer.

Hatano, G., & Inagaki, K. (1986). Two courses of expertise. In H. Stevenson, H. Azuma, & K. Hakuta (Eds.), *Child development and education in Japan* (pp. 262–272). New York, NY: Freeman.

Hattie, J. A. C. (2009). *Visible learning: A synthesis of over 800 meta-analyses relating to achievement.* New York, NY: Routledge.

Hattie, J. A. C. (2012). *Visible learning for teachers: Maximizing impact on learning.* New York, NY: Routledge.

Henniger, M. L. (2012). *Teaching young children: An introduction* (5th ed.). Upper Saddle River, NJ: Pearson.

Hille, K. (2011, June). Bringing research into educational practice: Lessons learned. *Mind, Brain, and Education, 5*(2), 63–70.

Hoy, W. K., Tarter, C. J., & Woolfolk Hoy, A. (2006). Academic optimism of schools: A force for student achievement. *American Educational Research Journal, 43*(3), 425–446.

Immordino-Yang, M. H. (2015, April). Embodied brains, social minds, cultural meaning: Applying social affective neuroscience to development and education. Presentation at American Educational Research Association 2015 Annual Meeting, Chicago, IL.

Immordino-Yang, M. H., & Damasio, A. (2007). We feel, therefore we learn: The relevance of affective and social neuroscience to education. *Mind, Brain, and Education, 1*(1), 3–10. doi:10.1111/j.1751-228X.2007.00004.x

Ingersol, R. M. (2005). The anomaly of educational organizations and the study of organizational control. In L. V. Hedges & B. Schneider (Eds.), *The social organization of schooling* (pp. 91–110). New York, NY: Russell Sage Foundation.

Jackson, P. W. (1990). *Life in classrooms.* New York, NY: Teachers College Press.

Johnson, J. (2012). *You can't do it alone: A communications and engagement manual for school leaders committed to reform.* Lanham, MD: Rowman & Littlefield Education.

Johnson, S. M., & Fiarman, S. E. (2012, November). The potential of peer review. *Educational Leadership, 70*(3), 20–25. Available at ascd.org/publications/educational-leadership/nov12/vol70/num03/The-Potential-of-Peer-Review.aspx

Johnson, S. M., Birkeland, S. E., Donaldson, M. L., Kardos, S. M., Kauffman, D., Liu, E., & Peske, H. G. (2004). *Finders and keepers: Helping new teachers survive and thrive in our schools.* San Francisco, CA: Jossey-Bass.

Katzenbach, J. R., & Smith, D. K. (2005, July–August). The discipline of teams. *Harvard Business Review.* Available at https://hbr.org/2005/07/the-discipline-of-teams

Katzenmeyer, M. H., & Moller, G. V. (2009). *Awakening the sleeping giant: Helping teachers develop as leaders* (3rd ed.). Thousand Oaks, CA: Corwin Press.

Kauchak, D. P., & Eggen, P. D. (2013). *Introduction to teaching: Becoming a professional* (5th ed.). Upper Saddle River, NJ: Pearson.

Kegan, R. (2000). What "form" transforms? A constructive-developmental approach to transformative learning. In J. Mezirow (Ed.), *Learning as transformation* (pp. 35–70). San Francisco, CA: Jossey-Bass.

Kegan, R., & Lahey, L. L. (2009). *Immunity to change: How to overcome it and unlock the potential in yourself and your organization* [Kindle version]. Boston, MA: Harvard Business School Press.

Kennedy, M. (2008). Teachers thinking about their practice. In T. Good (Ed.), *21st century education: A reference handbook* (Vol. 1, pp. 21–31). Thousand Oaks, CA: Sage. Available at sagepub.com/hall/study/materials/deeperlook/deeperlook1.7.pdf

Keyes, C. L. M. (1998, June). Social well-being. *Social Psychology Quarterly, 61*(2), 121–140.

Killingsworth, M. A., & Gilbert, D. T. (2010, November 12). A wandering mind is an unhappy mind. *Science*. doi:10.1126/science.1192439

Killion, J. (2013). *Establishing time for professional learning.* Oxford, OH: Learning Forward.

Kitchenham, A. (2008). The evolution of John Mezirow's transformative learning theory. *Journal of Transformative Learning, 6,* 104–124. doi:10.1177/1541344608322678

Knowles, M. S., Holton, E. F., & Swanson, R. A. (2005). *The adult learner: The definitive classic in adult education and human resource development* (6th ed.). London, UK: Elsevier.

Kolb, D. A. (1984). *Experiential learning: Experience as the source of learning and development.* Englewood Cliffs, NJ: Prentice Hall.

Kouzes, J. M., & Posner, B. Z. (2012). *The leadership challenge: How to make extraordinary things happen in organizations* (5th ed.). San Francisco, CA: Jossey-Bass.

Leana, C. R. (2011, Fall). The missing link in school reform. *Stanford Social Innovation Review*. Available at ssireview.org/articles/entry/the_missing_link_in_school_reform

Leonard, K., & Yorton, T. (2015). *Yes, and: How improvisation reverses "no, but" thinking and improves creativity and collaboration.* New York, NY: HarperBusiness.

Lieberman, A., & Friedrich, L. D. (2010). *How teachers become leaders: Learning from practice and research.* New York, NY: Teachers College Press.

Lieberman, M. D. (2012). Education and the social brain. *Trends in Neuroscience and Education, 1,* 3–9. Available at scn.ucla.edu/pdf/Lieberman(2012)TINE.pdf

Lieberman, M. D. (2013). *Social: Why our brains are wired to connect.* New York, NY: Crown.

Lillard, A., & Erisir, A. (2011). Old dogs learning new tricks: Neuroplasticity beyond the juvenile period. *Developmental Review, 31*(4), 207–239. Available at ncbi.nlm.nih.gov/pmc/articles/PMC3956134/

Lortie, D. (1975). *Schoolteacher: A sociological study.* Chicago, IL: University of Chicago Press.

Louis, K. S. (2006). *Organizing for school change: Contexts of learning.* New York, NY: Routledge.

Louis, K. S., Leithwood, K., Wahlstrom, K. L., & Anderson, S. E. (2010, July). *Learning from Leadership Project: Investigating the Links to Improved Student Learning.* New York, NY: Wallace Foundation. Available at wallacefoundation. org/knowledge-center/school-leadership/key-research/Documents/ Investigating-the-Links-to-Improved-Student-Learning.pdf

Lysaker, J., & Furuness, S. (2011). Space for transformation: Relational, dialogic pedagogy. *Journal of Transformative Education, 9*(3), 183–197.

Lyubomirsky, S. (2007). *The how of happiness: A new approach to getting the life you want.* New York, NY: Penguin.

Mendels, P. (2012, February). The effective principal. *JSD: The Learning Forward Journal, 33*(1), 54–58. Available at learningforward.org/docs/ february-2012/mendels331.pdf?sfvrsn=2

Merzenich, M. (2013). *Soft-wired: How the new science of brain plasticity can change your life.* San Francisco, CA: Parnassus.

Mezirow, J. (1990). *Fostering critical reflection in adulthood: A guide to transformative and emancipatory learning.* San Francisco, CA: Jossey-Bass.

Mischel, W. (2014). *The marshmallow test.* New York, NY: Little, Brown.

Moller, S., Mickelson, R. A., Stearns, E., Banerjee, N., & Bottia, M. C. (2013). Collective pedagogical teacher culture and mathematics achievement: Differences by race, ethnicity, and socioeconomic status. *Sociology of Education, 86*(2), 174. doi:10.1177/0038040712472911

National Council of Teachers of English. (2013). Formative assessment that truly informs assessment. Available at ncte.org/positions/statements/formative-assessment

Norcross, J. C. (2012). *Changeology: 5 steps to realizing your goals and resolutions.* New York, NY: Simon & Schuster.

Norman, P. J., & Feiman-Nemser, S. (2012). Mind activity in teaching and mentoring. *Teachers as learners* (pp. 277–306). Cambridge, MA: Harvard Education Press.

Oswald, A. J., Proto, E., & Sgroi, D. (2014, February 10). *Happiness and productivity* (3rd version). Available at http://www2.warwick.ac.uk/fac/ soc/economics/staff/eproto/workingpapers/happinessproductivity.pdf

Owens, E. (2015). Teacher leaders internationally. In N. Bond (Ed.), *The power of teacher leaders: Their roles, influence, and impact* (pp. 145–155). New York, NY: Routledge.

Painter, D. D. (n.d.). Teacher research could change your practice. Available at nea.org/tools/17289.htm

Pangan, C. H., & Lupton, A. (2015). First-year teachers: New and ready to lead. In N. Bond (Ed.), *The power of teacher leaders: Their roles, influence, and impact* (pp. 120–131). New York, NY: Routledge.

Pellegrino, J. W., & Hilton, M. L. (2012). *Education for life and work: Developing transferable knowledge and skills in the 21st century.* Washington, DC: National Academies Press.

Pentland, A. (2014). *Social physics: How good ideas spread.* New York, NY: Penguin.

Peterson, K. D., & Deal, T. E. (2009). *The shaping school culture fieldbook.* San Francisco, CA: Jossey-Bass.

Pryce-Jones, J. (2012, November 25). "Ways to be happy and productive at work." *The Wall Street Journal.* Available at blogs.wsj.com/source/2012/11/25/five-ways-to-be-happy-and-productive-at-work/

Reeves, D. B. (2008). *Reframing teacher leadership to improve your school.* Alexandria, VA: Association for Supervision and Curriculum Development.

Rogers, E. (2003). *Diffusion of innovations* (5th ed.). New York, NY: Free Press.

Rosenholtz, S. J. (1991). *Teachers' workplace: The social organization of schools.* Harlow, UK: Longman Group.

Safer, N., & Fleischman, S. (2005, February). Research matters: How student progress monitoring improves instruction. *Educational Leadership, 62*(5), 81–83. Available at ascd.org/publications/educational-leadership/feb05/vol62/num05/How-Student-Progress-Monitoring-Improves-Instruction.aspx

Sagor, R. (2000). *Guiding school improvement with action research.* Alexandria, VA: ASCD.

Sahlberg, P. (2011). *Finnish lessons: What can the world learn from educational change in Finland?* New York, NY: Teachers College Press.

Sahlberg, P. (2013, October). Teachers as leaders in Finland. *Educational Leadership, 71*(2), 36–40. Available at ascd.org/publications/educational-leadership/oct13/vol71/num02/Teachers-as-Leaders-in-Finland.aspx

Scholastic & the Bill and Melinda Gates Foundation. (2010). *Primary sources: America's teachers on America's schools.* Available at scholastic.com/primarysources/pdfs/Scholastic_Gates_0310.pdf

Schon, D. A. (1987). *Educating the reflective practitioner.* San Francisco, CA: Jossey Bass.

Seidler, R. D. (2012). Neuroplasticity in middle age: An ecologically valid approach. *Frontiers in Human Neuroscience, 6.* Available at ncbi.nlm.nih.gov/pmc/articles/PMC3509353/

Seligman, M. E. P. (2002). *Authentic happiness: Using the new positive psychology to realize your potential for lasting fulfillment.* New York, NY: Simon & Schuster.

Seligman, M. E. P. (2011a, April). Building resilience. *Harvard Business Review.* Available at hbr.org/2011/04/building-resilience/ar/1

Seligman, M. E. P. (2011b). *Flourish: A visionary new understanding of happiness and well-being.* New York, NY: Free Press.

Sherman, C. (2011, April 21). Improving memory to improve academic performance [Dana Foundation news release]. Available at dana.org/News/Details.aspx?id=43151

Smith, D., Wilson, B., & Corbett, D. (2009, February). Moving beyond talk. *Educational Leadership, 66*(5), 20–25. Available at ascd.org/publications/educational-leadership/feb09/vol66/num05/Moving-Beyond-Talk.aspx

Smylie, M. A., Miller, C. L., & Westbrook, K. P. (2008). The work of teachers. In T. Good (Ed.), *21st century education: A reference handbook* (Vol. 1, pp. 3–11). Thousand Oaks, CA: Sage.

Stix, G. (2014, July 14). Neuroplasticity: New clues to just how much the adult brain can change. *Talking Back* [*Scientific American* blog]. Available at blogs.scientificamerican.com/talking-back/2014/07/14/neuroplasticity-new-clues-to-just-how-much-the-adult-brain-can-change/

Stoll., L., McKay, J., & Kember, D., Cochorane-Smith, M., & Lytle, S. (1997). Spoon feeding leads to regurgitation: A better diet can result in more digestible learning outcomes. *Higher Education Research and Development, 16*(1), 55–67. Available at http://www.educationalleaders.govt.nz/Pedagogy-and-assessment/Leading-professional-learning/Teachers-as-learners

Study shows teacher collaboration, professional communities improve many elementary students' math scores. (2013, June 5). *Inside UNC Charlotte.* Available at inside.uncc.edu/news/item/study-shows-teacher-collaboration-professional-communities-improve-many-elementary-student

Sylwester, R. (2014, October). Credibility and validity of information. Part 1: Introduction. *Information Age Education Newsletter, 147.* Available at i-a-e.org/newsletters/IAE-Newsletter-2014-147.html

Teacher Leadership Exploratory Consortium. (n.d.) Teacher Leader Model Standards (TLMS). Available at teacherleaderstandards.org/downloads/TLS_Brochure.pdf

Tucker, M. S. (Ed.). (2011). *Surpassing Shanghai: An agenda for American education built on the world's leading systems.* Cambridge, MA: Harvard Education Press.

Tucker, M. S., & Ruzzi, B. B. (2011). Japan: Perennial league leader. In M. S. Tucker (Ed.), *Surpassing Shanghai: An agenda for American education built on the world's leading systems* (pp. 79–112). Cambridge, MA: Harvard Education Press.

Tucker, P. D., & Stronge, J. H. (2005). *Linking teacher evaluation and student learning.* Arlington, VA: ASCD.

Veenman, M. V. J. (2011). Learning to self-monitor and self-regulate. In R. E. Meyer & P. A. Alexander (Eds.), *Handbook of research on learning and instruction* (pp. 197–218). New York, NY: Routledge.

Waddell, J. H. (2010, May). Fostering relationships to increase teacher retention in urban schools. *Journal of Curriculum and Instruction, 4*(1), 70–85.

Wagner, T., & Kegen, R. (2006). *Change leadership: A practical guide to transforming our schools.* San Francisco, CA: Jossey-Bass.

Wang, M., Haertel, G., & Walberg, H. (1993). Toward a knowledge base for school learning. *Review of Educational Research, 63,* 249–294. doi:10.3102/00346543063003249

Watt, H. M. G., & Richardson, P. W. (2013). Teacher motivation and student achievement outcomes. In J. Hattie & E. M. Anderman (Eds.), *International guide to student achievement.* New York, NY: Routledge.

Weir, K. (2011, December). The exercise effect. *American Psychological Association Monitor, 42*(11). Available at apa.org/monitor/2011/12/exercise.aspx

Weisse, S. L., & Zentner, S. M. (2015). The impact of teacher leaders on students, colleagues, and communities: Insights from administrators. In N. Bond (Ed.), *The power of teacher leaders: Their roles, influence, and impact* (pp. 236–244). New York, NY: Routledge.

Welborn, B. (2012, October 3). Showing your work: How to change the public image of teaching. *Education Week.* Available at edweek.org/tm/articles/2012/10/03/tln_welborn_teaching.html

Wells, C. M., & Feun, L. (2013). Education change and professional learning communities: A study of two districts. *Journal of Educational Change, 14,* 233–257.

Willis, J. (2013). Cooperative learning: Accessing our highest human potential. In A. L. Costa & P. W. O'Leary (Eds.), *The power of the social brain: Teaching, learning, and interdependent thinking* (pp. 119–128). New York, NY: Teachers College Press.

Wilson, D. L., & Conyers, M. A. (2010). *Administrator's workbook for increasing student achievement: BrainSMART Strategies for leading and teaching.* Orlando, FL: BrainSMART.

Wilson, D. L., & Conyers, M. A. (2011a). *BrainSMART 60 strategies for increasing student learning* (4th ed.). Orlando, FL: BrainSMART.

Wilson, D. L., & Conyers, M. A. (2011b). *Thinking for results: Strategies for increasing student achievement by as much as 30 percent* (4th ed.). Orlando, FL: BrainSMART.

Wilson, D. L., & Conyers, M. A. (2013a). *Effective teaching, successful students* [Kindle version]. Orlando, FL: BrainSMART.

Wilson, D. L., & Conyers, M. A. (2013b). *Five big ideas for effective teaching: Connecting mind, brain, and education research to classroom practice.* New York, NY: Teachers College Press.

Wilson, N. S., & Bai, H. (2010). The relationship and impact of teachers' metacognitive knowledge and pedagogical understandings of metacognition. *Metacognition Learning*. Available at www4.ncsu.edu/~jlnietfe/Metacog_ Articles_files/Wilson%20%26%20Bai%20(2010).pdf

Woolfolk Hoy, A. (2012). Academic optimism and teacher education. *The Teacher Educator, 47*, 91–100. doi:10.1080/08878730.2012.662875

Woollett, K., & Maguire, E. A. (2011, December 20). Acquiring "the Knowledge" of London's layout drives structural brain changes. *Current Biology*, 2109– 2114. Available at ncbi.nlm.nih.gov/pmc/articles/PMC3268356/

Woolley, A. W., Chabris, C. F., Pentland, A., Hashmi, N., & Malone, T. W. (2010, September 30). Evidence for a collective intelligence factor in the performance of human groups. *Science*. doi:10.1126/science.1193147

York-Barr, J., & Duke, K. (2004). What do we know about teacher leadership? Findings from two decades of scholarship. *Review of Educational Research, 74*(3), 255–316. doi:10.3102/00346543074003255

York-Barr, J., Sommerness, J., & Hur, J. (2008). Teacher leadership. In T. L. Good (Ed.), *21st century education: A reference handbook* (Vol. 1, pp. 12– 20). Thousand Oaks, CA: Sage.

Zak, P. J. (2012, April 27). The trust molecule. *The Wall Street Journal*. Available at online.wsj.com/news/articles/SB10001424052702304811304577365 782995320366

Index

About the Authors

Marcus Conyers and **Donna Wilson**, PhD, are the co-developers of Master of Science and Educational Specialist degree programs with majors in Brain-Based Teaching and a concentration in Teacher Leadership, as well as a Doctorate in Education Minor in Brain-Based Leadership. They are the authors of 30 journal articles, book chapters, and books, including *Five Big Ideas for Effective Teaching: Connecting Mind, Brain, and Education Research to Classroom Practice.* Conyers serves as Director of Communications for the Center for Innovative Education and Prevention. Wilson, former chair of education at the University of Detroit Mercy, is a school and educational psychologist and adjunct professor at Nova Southeastern University.